Secrets of Slow Cooking

Secrets of Slow Cooking

CREATING EXTRAORDINARY FOOD WITH YOUR SLOW COOKER

LIANA KRISSOFF   PHOTOGRAPHS BY KIRSTEN STRECKER

Stewart, Tabori & Chang • New York

Library of Congress Cataloging-in-Publication Data
Krissoff, Liana.
    Secrets of slow cooking : creating extraordinary food with your slow
cooker / Liana Krissoff; photographs by Kirsten Strecker.
        p. cm.
    Includes index.
    ISBN–13: 978-1-58479-441-7
    ISBN–10: 1-58479-441-0
    1. Electric cookery, Slow. I. Title.

TX827.K75 2005
    641.5'884—dc22   2005048970

Published in 2005 by
Stewart, Tabori & Chang
An imprint of Harry N. Abrams, Inc.

Printed and bound in China

10 9 8 7 6 5 4

HNA ■■■■■
harry n. abrams, inc.
a subsidiary of La Martinière Groupe

115 West 18th Street
New York, NY 10011
www.hnabooks.com

ACKNOWLEDGMENTS

I'd like to thank, first, Marisa Bulzone, my editor, for her encouragement and for her smart, thoughtful guidance through every stage of this book's development and production. I also thank the people who made the book look as good as it does—Kirsten Strecker and Heather Anne Thomas; Julie Hoffer; Michael Pederson, Tracy Harlor, and Darius Marter; and Lynda White. Thanks to Leda Scheintaub, the copyeditor, and Sylvia Karchmar, the proofreader, for their invaluable suggestions and corrections.

I owe a great debt to my mom, Diana Fredley, a constant source of always-dead-on advice—I thank her especially for allowing me to crib her excellent roti, fesenjen, and koresh recipes. Finally I want to thank my husband, Derek, for just everything.

CONTENTS

INTRODUCTION

A slow cooker allows you to cook foods at low temperatures for long periods of time. Tough cuts of meat become tender, vegetables cook so slowly that they don't turn to mush before the meat is done, beans soften evenly, spices mellow, and flavors meld together seamlessly. Because the heating elements are enclosed in a protective housing, you can leave it on while you're away from the kitchen or even away from the house entirely. There's usually no need to tend to the food at all as it cooks, so in many cases you can put the ingredients in the cooker in the morning, let it simmer all day while you do other things, and supper will be ready in the evening.

Slow-cooker cookbooks used to focus on this convenience at the expense of just about every other reason to cook your own food—flavor, texture, freshness... okay, I'll say it: soulfulness. Throw everything in the cooker and eat what comes out at the end of the day. This cookbook is different. There might be a few more steps involved in these recipes, but the ingredients are, well, pure (no canned sliced mushrooms), for the most part the dishes are ones that are best done in a slow cooker (I admit that there are a few dishes here for which convenience is the main reason a slow cooker is used—the mashed potatoes on page 36 is one example), and what comes out is pretty darned delicious by any standard.

CHOOSING A SLOW COOKER

Size: Slow cookers are available in just about any size, from the smallest 16-ounce "Little Dipper" Crock-Pot made by Rival, which doesn't cook but merely warms up foods, to the enormous and beautiful 7-quart All-Clad stainless-steel-housed cooker. The most common sizes are in the 4- to 5-quart range: A 4-quart pot can be used to make enough ribollita (page 79), for example, to generously serve about 4 people; or enough rendang padang (page 82), say, to serve 6 with rice on the side. These midsize workhorse models are the cookers you could use every day (if you were insane, or writing a cookbook of slow-cooker foods, which in the end amounts to about the same thing). For larger groups, or to make big batches of food for freezing or canning, a 6½- or 7-quart slow cooker is the one for the job, and in some cases only this larger size makes sense—if you're baking the brownies on

smudged, water-spotted one—and that slow cooker is going to get dripped on, finger-printed, and smeared after a single use, no matter how obsessively neat you are. Invest in a bottle of stainless-steel cleaner or an all-purpose polish like Nevr-Dull.

OTHER USEFUL EQUIPMENT

Immersion (Stick) Blender: These little handheld blenders can be used to puree soups flawlessly, thicken chowders and bean dishes instantly, mash potatoes—and some, like the Russell Hobbs model, even come with a cream-whipping attachment. They eliminate the need to transfer soup contents to a regular blender, in batches, and then back to the pot to reheat, because you can blend the ingredients right in the pot. The metal parts, however, can scratch the surface of the crockery, so use a light hand when moving the blender around in the insert, and try not to let it come in contact with the bottom or sides.

Blenders: A blender can be used to puree easy vegetable soups, like the velvety butternut squash soup on page 54, and to thicken too-runny cooking liquids (spoon some of the soft vegetables in a pot roast or some of the beans in the basic black bean recipe on page 37, for example, into the blender, puree for a few seconds, then return the puree to the cooker). A blender is used, too, for pureeing the tomatillos and other ingredients in the mole verde on page 98, and for the chile puree in the posole on page 63. A pulse button and low and high speeds are essential features (to avoid splattering, start blending warm mixtures on the lowest speed, then increase the speed to high to finish pureeing), and are standard on even the most basic blenders.

Food Processors: I use a food processor for several dishes in this book. It's the best tool for making the spice paste for the doro wat on page 99, chopping the walnuts for the fesenjen on page 96, and making the Indonesian curry paste for the rendang padang on page 82. Either a full-size food processor or a mini food processor will work well, but in most cases I've found that the smaller size is best: The ingredients in the pastes and sauces become incorporated more quickly and become more evenly pureed in a smaller work bowl. A mini food processor also makes easy work of homemade mayonnaise, fresh herb sauces, and aioli. Of course, if you want to make larger batches of the spice pastes or sauces in this book to freeze for later, use a full-size food processor. As with blenders, look for a food processor with low and high speeds, and a pulse button. Most larger models (and they come in sizes up to 16 cups) have wide feed tubes and several different blade attachments for shredding, grating, slicing, and chopping, as well as plastic blades for kneading dough.

Heavy Skillet or Sauté Pan: So that you don't have to work in several batches when you brown ingredients before adding them to the slow cooker, a nice big pan will be most useful. It also helps if your pan is nonstick or at least well seasoned so you don't have to use too much oil or other fat during browning—and in the palak paneer recipe on page 46 a well-seasoned pan is downright essential for browning the cheese cubes.

Meat Grinder and Sausage Stuffer: Grinding your own meat means you can grind it as finely or coarsely as required for each dish you make, and use meat that you know is fresh and as fatty or lean as you like. And stuffing your own sausages—while hardly fix-it-and-etc.—expands the possibilities of a slow cooker immensely. Whether you are buying a dedicated meat grinder and sausage stuffer or the corresponding attachments to a stand mixer, there are a few things to think about: How easy or difficult will all the parts be to clean? How fine and coarse are the different blades or plates? On my husband's heavy-duty Waring grinder, the finest disk has holes that are about 3.5 millimeters in diameter, which happens to yield beef that's just the right texture for Cincinnati-style chili (page 70). Can different sizes of casings be used with the sausage-stuffing attachment, or is there more than one size of sausage stuffer? Making a thick sausage with a narrow stuffer can be an awkward process. finally, do you have someone to help you stuff sausages? I'm not the most coordinated person I know, and I'm not able to keep the meat going in at an even rate while holding the casing to make sure it's being stuffed evenly—it really is a two-person job.

Tongs and a Slotted Spoon: Sounds a little obvious, maybe, but when I was developing the recipes for this book, my one pair of stainless-steel spring-loaded tongs got more use than just about any other tool in my ridiculously well-stocked utensil drawers, so I thought I'd mention them here. Often when making food in a slow cooker you'll notice that a big hunk of meat is done but the liquidy sauce is still too, well, liquidy: Just pull out the meat with the tongs, pour the juices into a saucepan, and boil the juices until they're thickened to your liking, then transfer everything back to the cooker to heat through. Also, I like to cook chicken on the bone and then pull out the bones after it's cooked, and this task is made much easier with a good pair of tongs. A slotted spoon will work just fine for the same purposes.

Slow-Cooking Tips and Techniques

Every slow cooker sold nowadays comes with a little booklet full of dos and don'ts, hints and warnings. Most of them are perfectly reasonable, and deal with food safety issues. (It's best not to cook whole chickens unless you know that your cooker is powerful enough to bring foods to a boil relatively quickly, because the insides won't come up to contaminate-killing temperature soon enough. Don't reheat refrigerated foods in the slow cooker. Start with mostly room-temperature ingredients. Let the crockery insert cool down a bit before washing it so it doesn't crack. And so on.) But many of them, I've found, are misleading or just plain weird. (Says one owner's manual: "Wipe meats well to remove residue." What residue?) Here are some basic practices to keep in mind.

Choosing Main Ingredients: Use meats that are well marbled and not too lean—the long cooking time will break down the connective tissue in the meat and make the meat tender and keep it moist; lean cuts (loin, for example) will become tough and dry. If you're using ground meat, it can be as lean or fatty as you'd like: Just brown it first and drain off the fat. Don't slow-cook chicken breasts (the texture after cooking is truly awful, like a crumbcake but vaguely chicken-flavored); use trimmed and skinned thighs and legs, or wings, instead.

Just about any vegetable, grain, or legume—potatoes, hard squashes, carrots, celery, greens, polenta, wild or brown rice, beans—can be slow-cooked. Some more tender vegetables—snow peas, asparagus, peas—should only be added in the last 30 minutes, or quickly steamed on the stovetop and folded into the dish at the last minute.

Browning: In most of the meat recipes I suggest browning the meat on the stovetop before adding it to the slow cooker. Except in the case of ground meat, which should always be precooked to reduce the risk of contamination, browning is not strictly necessary; however, it does allow you to drain off excess fat from less-lean meats, and I think the browning results in a deeper, richer flavor and color. Sometimes I indicate that vegetables should be browned or slightly softened first on the stovetop in some oil or other fat. Again, this is optional; I've just found that without the extra fat and golden-brown bits a vegetable-based soup can taste a bit thin. For the same reason, in these recipes you'll notice that often part of the liquid for the dish is added to the browning skillet so that those browned bits in the pan can be scraped up and included in the dish.

Seasonings: I don't know why instruction booklets tell you that spices and strong flavorings "intensify" while they're in the slow cooker, because the opposite seems to be true in most cases. Garlic, for example, becomes much more subtle after several hours in the slow cooker—so either use a lot of it, or lightly sauté it in a pan and add it at the end. Pepper, cumin, cinnamon, ground cayenne, and even reconstituted and pureed dried hot chiles (as in the posole on page 63) should be used liberally. As should salt—add it toward the end of cooking, a little bit at a time, tasting after each addition.

Just as with most stovetop- or oven-cooked dishes that require long simmering, fresh herbs should be added at the end of the cooking time or they'll turn black. I add whole fresh basil sprigs to the marinara sauce on page 49 at the very beginning of the cooking, to infuse the long-cooked sauce with basil flavor, but the sprigs are pulled out and discarded and fresh basil added at the end. Another solution is to put fresh herb sprigs in a cheesecloth bag and nestle it into the other ingredients while they cook; remove and discard the bag before serving.

You might notice that the amount of onion in these recipes seems small compared to similar conventional recipes. When I first started using a slow cooker many of my concoctions had a strong and not entirely pleasant flavor that I couldn't quite place. It took me a while to isolate the culprit: too much onion. I'm not sure why, but the slow cooker seems to trap the oniony flavor and odor more than a regular covered pot; also, of course, onions release a heck of a lot of liquid, and in slow cooking excess liquid's your enemy. So here I use about half the amount of onion I'd use if cooking a dish on the stovetop or in the oven.

Lifting the Lid: The thing about using a slow cooker is that you don't have to watch the pot or stir or otherwise disturb the ingredients. But that doesn't mean you *mustn't* do all that. Go ahead and lift the lid—part of cooking is seeing what's going on in the pot, tasting it, adding ingredients. Sure, heat is lost, and for most dishes you should keep the lid on as much as possible, but I've found that the food comes back up to temperature fairly quickly after the lid has been briefly removed. So don't worry too much about it.

Thickening: Runniness of stews and sauces is really not that much of an issue in these dishes. There are only a couple of recipes in this book (the fesenjen on page 96 is one) in which the sauce has become so liquidy by the end of the cooking time that something extra needs to be done about it (the walnut-pomegranate sauce for the fesenjen is simmered in the pan on the stovetop to reduce and thicken it). None of my recipes uses the cornstarch that's ubiquitous in the crockery-cookery tomes of old. I simply use less liquid (and less onion) to begin with, or brown the ingredients with a little flour first, as in a conventional recipe (see the chicken and dumplings on page 93, for example), or smash some of the vegetables against the side of the crockery insert to thicken the liquid slightly (the black beans on page 37). To thicken the red beans on page 76, I make a slurry of some of the liquid and a little flour and stir it into the beans at the end, just as I saw one of the best cooks I've ever met do when he made the same dish on his stove in Louisiana. And in the recipe for beef and sweet potato stew on page 67 I add, filipino-style, finely ground toasted rice to thicken the juices—try this if you're adapting one of your own recipes and are at a loss for thickening agents.

Using Dairy: It's true what they say: Milk, cream, and cheese should be added only in the last hour of cooking, or strange things will happen—curdling, separating, and general weirdness. (This is why I've used coconut milk instead of regular milk in the rice pudding on page 110—it just happens to taste good too.) In my efforts to keep these slow-cooker dishes as much like their conventional-pot counterparts as possible, I've avoided using the prepared or processed ingredients that are commonly used in slow-cooker recipes to substitute for dairy products: You'll find no canned cream-of-anything soup here, no evaporated or condensed milk.

Washing Up: The crockery insert and glass lid can be removed from the housing after it's cooled for an hour or so and cleaned with a dishrag or nylon scrubber brush with hot, soapy water. If food sticks to the sides, let it soak for a few hours. Don't use abrasive cleansers or anything that might scratch the surface (wire brushes and the like). Clean the housing inside and out with a damp dishrag.

NOTES ON THE RECIPES

Almost all of the recipes here were developed and tested in a standard 4-quart oval slow cooker, and cooked on the low setting for most of the cooking time to allow the cook more flexibility during the day. These recipes will, however, work just as well in 3½- or 5-quart cookers, with no significant adjustments to amounts or cooking time—again, this very-low-heat style of cooking is extremely forgiving; cooking a stew for a little more or less time isn't going to make much difference. If you'd like to use a larger (6- to 7-quart) cooker, either *double the recipe* (as long as the cooker isn't filled more than three quarters full, you're fine) or *reduce the cooking time* by about one third. If time is short, or if the food doesn't seem to be cooking quickly enough and people are getting hungry, you can cook on the high setting: In general, *2 hours on low equals 1 hour on high*.

One important issue to note is that slow cookers do vary, and one may cook significantly more slowly than another. In addition, variations in household voltage apparently affect the amount of heat generated in the pot. My mom has to cook dishes at least a couple of hours longer than I do, even though our slow cookers are the same size and we're using the same recipes.

APPETIZERS & PARTY FOODS

SPICY SOY-GLAZED SHORT RIBS

Serves 6 as an appetizer
4-quart slow cooker

3½ pounds beef short ribs

2 bunches scallions, trimmed and thinly sliced on the diagonal

1 clove garlic, minced

1 1-inch piece fresh ginger, peeled and minced

⅓ cup soy sauce

¼ cup rice vinegar

¼ cup molasses

¼ cup brown sugar

¼ cup chili-garlic sauce (see Note)

¼ cup plum or hoisin sauce (optional)

Juice of 2 limes

1 tablespoon toasted-sesame oil

1 teaspoon cayenne pepper

½ teaspoon freshly ground black pepper

2 tablespoons sesame seeds

These ribs can be served as a snack or party dish, hot or at room temperature. They're also good warmed up the next day in a 375°F oven for 15 minutes. To make this a main-course dish, serve the ribs over steamed white rice, with more of the sauce spooned over the rice.

Trim any excess fat or sinew off the ribs. In a heavy skillet over medium-high heat, brown half of the ribs well on all sides, about 8 minutes total, then remove the ribs to a 4-quart slow cooker (they will fit better in an oval cooker); repeat with the remaining ribs. Pour ½ cup water into the skillet and scrape up all the browned bits in the bottom of the pan. Pour the liquid over the ribs in the cooker.

In a medium bowl, combine half of the scallions and all the remaining ingredients except the sesame seeds, stirring until the brown sugar is dissolved. Pour the mixture over the ribs. Cook, covered, on the low setting for 4 hours, or until the meat is very tender and almost falling off the bones.

In a small skillet over medium-high heat, toast the sesame seeds, shaking the skillet and stirring constantly, until they just begin to color. Transfer to a small bowl and set aside.

Remove the ribs from the sauce and place on a large serving platter or on individual plates. Spoon a little of the sauce over the ribs and sprinkle with the sesame seeds and the remaining scallions. Serve.

Note: Chili-garlic sauce is a chunky red-chile sauce that can be found in the Asian-foods section of most supermarkets.

Pictured on page 18

DUCK CONFIT

Makes about 2 cups meat
4-quart slow cooker

About ¼ cup salt

1   shallot, minced

½   bunch fresh thyme sprigs

4   duck legs with thighs
    About 2½ cups rendered
    duck or goose fat
    Vegetable oil or light olive oil,
    if necessary

We should all be making more duck confit, the juicy, dark, long-cooked leg meat that's an essential ingredient in Rillettes (page 23) and Cassoulet (page 72) and excellent in pasta dishes and salads. With a slow cooker it couldn't be easier, and the uses to which this rich meat can be put are endless. And at least at my local butcher, Esposito Pork Shop, fresh duck legs aren't as expensive as you might expect. The duck or goose fat, to be honest, isn't cheap (a 24-ounce can of it runs twelve dollars in my neighborhood); however, it can be reused many times: Just strain any extra liquid fat back into the can and keep it at room temperature. There'll be a layer of meat juices on the bottom when the fat solidifies, but I've found that you can just dump all of it—fat and juices—into the slow cooker with the next batch of duck legs and the confit won't suffer in the least.

Sprinkle half of the salt in a shallow glass or plastic container, then sprinkle with half of the shallot and half of the thyme. Lay the duck legs, fat side up, in one layer over the salt mixture, then sprinkle the remaining salt, shallot, and thyme over them. Cover and refrigerate for at least 1 day or up to 2 days.

Rinse off the duck legs and pat them dry with paper towels. Place them in a 4-quart slow cooker in one snug layer (they can overlap slightly). Pour in the fat to just cover the duck legs, adding oil if necessary. Cook, covered, on the low setting for 5 to 6 hours, until the fat is darker and caramel colored and the meat can be easily pulled from the bones.

Using tongs, remove the duck legs from the fat and take the meat off the bones. The confit can be used right away or stored for future use. To store: Put the meat in a sealable container and cover them completely with the fat. Let cool, then cover the container and keep in the refrigerator for up to several weeks, making sure that you re-cover the meat with fat after removing any of it.

RILLETTES

Makes enough to fill 4 small ramekins

2   generous cups meat from
    about 4 legs Duck Confit
    (page 21)

1   small shallot, minced

½   teaspoon fresh thyme
    leaves, minced

    Generous pinch freshly
    grated nutmeg

    About ½ cup liquid fat from
    duck confit

    Toast points, thinly sliced
    baguette, or apple chips
    for serving

4   small sprigs fresh thyme
    (optional), for garnish

Little ramekins of this simple, rich spread—made with your own slow-cooked confit—make excellent gifts: The rillettes will keep for weeks as long as the surface is covered with a layer of fat.

Put the duck meat, shallot, minced thyme, and nutmeg in a food processor and pulse until the meat is fairly evenly shredded but not pureed. Transfer the mixture to a medium bowl and stir in about 3 tablespoons of the fat—just enough to bind the ingredients together in a thick, slightly chunky paste. Serve the rillettes at room temperature, spread on toast points, thin slices of baguette, or apple chips. To store, pack the rillettes into ramekins and smooth the top; spoon a ¼-inch layer of fat onto the surface and lay a thyme sprig in the fat, if desired. The ramekins can be stored in the refrigerator for several weeks.

JERK CHICKEN WINGS

Serves 4
4-quart slow cooker

3 pounds chicken wings

4 to 6 Scotch bonnet chiles,
   stemmed, seeded, and
   chopped

6 scallions, white and green
   parts, chopped

2 cloves garlic, chopped

6 sprigs fresh thyme, tough
   stems removed

⅓ cup whole allspice berries,
   finely ground

3 tablespoons rum

3 tablespoons brown sugar, plus
   more to taste if necessary

1½ teaspoons salt, plus more to
   taste if necessary

½ teaspoon freshly ground
   black pepper, plus more to
   taste if necessary

3 tablespoons vegetable oil
   About 2 tablespoons honey
   (optional)

These Caribbean-influenced wings are a bit sweet and very spicy. Be careful when working with Scotch bonnet chiles: Wear plastic gloves and don't touch your eyes.

Chop off the chicken wing tips; discard them or save them for making stock. Cut each wing in half at the joint. Place the pieces in a 4-quart slow cooker.

In a food processor or blender, combine all the remaining ingredients except the honey and process to a smooth, barely pourable paste. Scrape the paste into the cooker and toss to coat the wings. Cook, covered, on the low setting for 4 to 6 hours, until the wings are tender but not quite falling off the bones.

Preheat the oven to 425°F. Using tongs, remove the chicken wings from the cooker and arrange them on a nonstick sheet pan in one layer so that the pieces aren't touching one another. Drizzle the honey, if using, over the wings. Bake for 15 minutes, or until the wings are crisp and starting to brown. Serve the wings hot or at room temperature.

TWO-CHEESE ARTICHOKE DIP

Makes about 2½ cups
16-ounce slow cooker

2   (14-ounce) cans artichoke
    hearts (about 10), well drained

½   cup freshly grated Parmesan
    cheese

2   ounces butter kase or other
    flavorful semisoft cheese, cut
    into bits

½   cup mayonnaise

1   large fresh jalapeño chile,
    stemmed, seeded, and
    thinly sliced

2   tablespoons heavy cream

This makes enough for two batches of dip when made in a very small 16-ounce slow cooker; you can keep the second batch in the refrigerator, covered, for about a day. Butter kase has a deep nutty flavor and melts smoothly; substitute a good plain havarti, or chaumes, Pont L'Evêque, or a firm taleggio.

Roughly chop the artichoke hearts and combine them with all the remaining ingredients, stirring to break up the artichokes and butter kase a bit. Spoon about half of the mixture into a 16-ounce mini slow cooker and warm for 1 to 2 hours, until the cheese is melted and the jalapeño has softened. Serve with tortilla chips or toasted pita or chapati wedges, leaving the cooker on but removing the lid.

BLACK BEAN DIP

Makes about 1½ cups
16-ounce slow cooker

1½ cups drained Basic Black
    Beans (page 37)

4   ounces Monterey Jack cheese,
    shredded

2 or 3 fresh hot chiles, stemmed,
    seeded, and minced

¼   cup chopped fresh cilantro

¼   teaspoon ground cumin

    Juice of ½ lime

    Tortilla chips to serve

This is an easy, quick dip to make for a party or informal get-together. Keep the dip in the slow cooker—it'll stay warm and gooey throughout the evening. The dip is also good with toasted split pita or chapati wedges.

Puree the beans in a blender or food processor until chunky-smooth, to yield a consistency like thick rice pudding. Stir in the cheese, chiles, cilantro, cumin, and lime juice. Fill a 16-ounce mini slow cooker with the mixture and warm for 1 hour, until the cheese is melted; serve with tortilla chips, directly from the slow cooker to keep the dip warm.

CURRIED ALMONDS

Makes 2½ cups
4-quart slow cooker

2½ cups shelled almonds

¼ cup butter, melted

2 teaspoons curry powder

1 teaspoon salt

1 teaspoon ground cumin

½ teaspoon cayenne pepper

¼ teaspoon freshly ground
    black pepper

These simple, buttery, toasty nuts are an excellent accompaniment to strong cold or hot cocktails.

Combine all the ingredients in a 4-quart slow cooker and cook, covered, on the low setting for 4 hours. Uncover and cook on the high setting for about 1 hour, until some of the nuts begin to brown and develop cracks; then remove the nuts to a plate to cool. Serve at room temperature.

CAPONATA

Serves 4 to 6
as an appetizer or antipasto
4-quart slow cooker

2   medium eggplants

4   ribs celery

1   cup pitted black or green olives,
     or a combination

2   tablespoons drained capers

1   (28-ounce) can peeled chopped
     Italian tomatoes, with juices

¼   cup red-wine or cider vinegar,
     or a combination of cider and
     balsamic vinegars

2   tablespoons brown sugar

2   tablespoons extra-virgin olive oil

4   cloves garlic, chopped
     Salt and freshly ground black
     pepper

⅓   cup golden raisins

¼   cup pine nuts or chopped
     blanched almonds, toasted

1   cup fresh basil leaves, sliced
     into thin ribbons

¼   cup fresh parsley leaves, chopped

Caponata is a classic component of an antipasto plate, or can be spooned on top of thick slices of bruschetta; it also makes an excellent lunch with a couple of chunks of good crusty bread, maybe a wedge of hard cheese, some greens lightly dressed with just olive oil, salt, and pepper, accompanied by a glass of spicy red wine.

Cut the eggplant into ½-inch or larger chunks and put them in a 4-quart slow cooker. Slice the celery into ½-inch lengths and add them to the cooker, along with the olives, capers, and tomatoes. Combine the vinegar and brown sugar and stir to dissolve the sugar, then pour the mixture over the vegetables in the cooker.

Put the oil and garlic in a small sauté pan and place over medium heat; cook, stirring frequently, until the garlic is fragrant and softened but not browned, about 4 minutes. Scrape the oil and garlic into the cooker, season lightly with salt and pepper, and toss to combine all the ingredients.

Cook, covered, on the low setting for 4 hours, or until the celery is tender. If the caponata is too runny, uncover the cooker and turn the setting to high for the last 30 minutes of the cooking time.

Stir in the raisins, pine nuts, basil, and parsley and cook until the raisins are plump, about 10 minutes. Season to taste with salt and pepper and serve warm or at room temperature.

ACHAR (INDONESIAN QUICK PICKLES)

Serves 6 to 8 as an accompaniment

1   cucumber
1   carrot
½   red onion
1   cup thinly sliced white cabbage
    (optional)
1   clove garlic, halved
2   fresh Serrano chiles, halved
1   tablespoon salt
¼   cup white vinegar
2   tablespoons sugar

Cut the cucumber, carrot, and onion into julienne strips. Place in a bowl with the cabbage, garlic, chiles, and salt and toss to combine well. Let stand at room temperature for 30 minutes. Turn the vegetables out into a colander and rinse under cold running water to remove the salt; drain well.

In a small saucepan, heat the vinegar, ¼ cup water, and the sugar until the sugar is dissolved and the liquid is boiling. Immediately pour the mixture over the vegetables in the bowl and toss to combine. Cover and refrigerate for at least 3 hours or overnight. Serve cold.

VEGETABLES, SIDES & SAUCES

COLLARD GREENS & THE BEST CORNBREAD MUFFINS

Serves 4 to 6
6-quart slow cooker

2 pounds collard greens
1 large smoked ham hock or
   smoked pork neckbone
½ small onion, diced
3 cloves garlic, smashed
2 dried hot chiles, stemmed
   Salt and freshly ground
   black pepper
   Hot-pepper-infused vinegar
   Best Cornbread Muffins
   (recipe follows)

Makes 10

1 cup all-purpose flour
1 cup yellow cornmeal
4 teaspoons baking powder
1 tablespoon sugar
1 teaspoon salt
1 large egg
1 cup whole milk
4 tablespoons butter, melted

Pictured on page 32

I used to be one of those people who undercook collard greens—you know, al dente and all. I'm not sure what made me realize my folly, but at some point I grew up and started cooking them right—that is, overcooking *them. And nothing's better at reducing vegetables, collards included, to the very tender stage than a slow cooker.*

Wash the greens and pull off and discard any tough, thick stems. Tear the leaves into pieces about the size of your palm. Put the greens, ham hock, onion, garlic, and chiles in a 6-quart slow cooker and add about 5 cups water, enough to come about halfway up the side of the cooker. Cook, covered, on the high setting for 6 to 8 hours, until the greens are very, very soft and the meat is tender. Using tongs, remove the ham hock and pull off the meat, discarding the bones and fat. Return the meat to the cooker. Cook, uncovered, on the high setting for another 30 minutes. Season generously with salt and pepper to taste and serve hot, with the vinegar and muffins on the side.

Best Cornbread Muffins

When Derek, the guy I'd marry a few months later, came to visit me in Italy, he gave me the best birthday present I've ever received: a little notebook in which he'd pasted photographs of soul food and barbecue restaurants around Athens, Georgia, where he lived at the time; opposite the pictures, he'd written out recipes he'd collected from people he'd met during his time in the south. I turned straight to this recipe (only slightly adjusted here), from Cheryl Berzanskis, of Pampa, Texas, got out the coarse polenta and doppio-zero flour, cracked a bright-yellow egg from a friend's mother's hen, and made up a batch. You'd think cornbread would be a no-brainer, but for some reason I'd always had problems making it to my liking: I like it corny, rough, and savory—not sweet at all. But even using hard Italian flour, and no measuring cups, that was the best cornbread I've ever eaten, much less made myself.

Preheat the oven to 425°F.

In a medium bowl, whisk together the flour, cornmeal, baking powder, sugar, and salt.

In a separate small bowl, whisk together the egg, milk, and butter. Pour the egg mixture into the flour mixture and use a spatula or spoon to gently combine them, stirring just until the dry ingredients are moistened; do not overmix.

Spoon the batter into a 12-cup nonstick muffin tin, filling the holes three quarters full, and filling the 2 empty holes with water to prevent them from burning. Bake for 15 to 20 minutes, until the tops of the muffins are just beginning to brown at the edges. Let the muffins cool in the tin for a few minutes, then tip out the water and remove the muffins from the tin. Serve warm, or let cool to room temperature; the muffins will keep, in an airtight container, for 1 day—refresh them in a warm oven if desired.

HERBED MASHED POTATOES

Serves 4
4-quart slow cooker

2   pounds russet potatoes
    (about 4), quartered
1¼ cups whole milk
3   tablespoons butter
2   teaspoons salt
½   cup chopped mixed herbs
    such as basil, parsley, thyme,
    and chives

Here the advantage of using a slow cooker is simply that you can let the potatoes cook while you're away from the house for a few hours. If you want the cooking to take longer, cook the potatoes whole, or in larger pieces. The potatoes can be peeled or not, as is your preference.

Put the potatoes in a 4-quart slow cooker and cover with cold water. Cook, covered, on the low setting for 4 to 5 hours, until the potatoes are very tender. Drain and return the potatoes to the cooker; turn the cooker to the high setting and leave the lid off to dry out the potatoes while you heat the milk.

In a small saucepan, heat the milk, butter, and salt over low heat until the butter is just melted; do not let the milk boil—it should be just steaming. Pour the mixture over the potatoes and mash with a potato masher to the desired consistency (use a plastic masher to avoid scratching the surface of the cooker insert). Fold in the herbs and serve hot.

Garlic Mashed Potatoes
For garlic mashed potatoes, simply add 1 head roasted garlic to the potatoes after they're drained. A whole head sounds like a lot, but I figure if you're going to make garlic mashed potatoes you might as well make them garlicky. Leave the potato skins on, and add lots of freshly ground black pepper. To roast garlic, slice a head in half crosswise and put it in a small baking dish or custard cup; drizzle with olive oil and sprinkle with salt and pepper. Cover with aluminum foil and roast at 350°F for about 1 hour, until the garlic cloves are soft and caramel colored. Squeeze the garlic pulp from the skins before using.

Pictured with Salmon with Baby Zucchini & Basil on page 102

BASIC BLACK BEANS

Serves 4
4-quart slow cooker

½ onion, diced

1 clove garlic, chopped

1 bay leaf

½ teaspoon cayenne pepper

1 tablespoon dried epazote leaves (optional)

2 cups dried black beans, rinsed and picked over

Salt and freshly ground black pepper

1 tablespoon sweet sherry (oloroso)

For black bean soup:

4 teaspoons Mexican *crema*, sour cream, or thick heavy cream

4 tablespoons crumbled cotija cheese (*queso anejado*)

4 sprigs fresh cilantro, for garnish

You can make a big pot of these beans, then use them in any of three ways: serve them just as they are, over plain white rice; puree them to make a very refined and elegant black bean soup; or use them to make Black Bean Dip (page 28). They can also be put in small containers and frozen for up to several months.

Place the onion, garlic, bay leaf, cayenne, the epazote (if using) and the beans in a 4-quart slow cooker. Pour in enough water to cover the ingredients by 1½ inches. Cook, covered, on the low setting for 8 to 9 hours, until the beans are soft.

To serve as basic black beans: Spoon out some of the cooking liquid and discard, then mash some of the beans against the side of the pot to thicken slightly. Season to taste with salt and pepper, then stir in the sherry and serve.

To serve as a soup: Spoon some of the cooking liquid into a cup, then use an immersion (stick) blender to puree the beans until smooth. (Alternatively, use a regular blender and puree the soup in batches.) If necessary, stir in some of the reserved liquid to yield a soup with the desired thickness. Season to taste with salt and pepper. Ladle the soup into wide shallow soup plates and drizzle the sherry and *crema* over the top. Sprinkle with the cotija, garnish with the cilantro sprigs, and serve.

EGGPLANT TIAN

Serves 4
4-quart slow cooker

1   large onion
4   cloves garlic
    Salt and freshly ground
    black pepper
2   large sprigs fresh basil,
    stemmed (about ½ cup leaves)
4   roasted red bell peppers,
    peeled, seeded, and stemmed
    (see Notes)
1½ pounds eggplant (about 1½
    large eggplants)
⅓   cup extra-virgin olive oil
¼   cup freshly grated
    Parmesan cheese
¼   cup dry bread crumbs
    (optional)

One of my favorite vegetable recipes is Linda Dannenberg's eggplant tian in Fresh Herb Cooking *(Stewart, Tabori & Chang, 2001), but the oven version in her book does take a fair amount of tending during a long cooking time. The results from a slow cooker are just as good, I think, and the process requires very little actual effort.*

Slice the onion vertically into ½-inch slivers and place in a 4-quart slow cooker. Smash the garlic and sprinkle the pieces over the onion. Sprinkle lightly with salt and pepper to taste. Arrange the basil in a layer to completely cover the onion, then top with half of the roasted peppers, laid flat over the basil.

Peel the eggplant and slice it into ½-inch-thick rounds. Arrange half of the slices, overlapping, in a single layer over the roasted peppers in the cooker. Lay the remaining roasted peppers over the eggplant and top with a final layer of eggplant slices. Sprinkle with salt and pepper, then drizzle the oil over all. Cook on the low setting, covered, for 6 to 8 hours, until the layers have sunk down and the top layer of eggplant is extremely soft and just barely holds its shape; do not stir.

Preheat the broiler. Keeping the vegetables in layers with the onion on the bottom, use a large spoon to transfer them, with a bit of their juices, to a 9½-inch square or round baking dish. Sprinkle with the cheese and the bread crumbs (if using) and drizzle with some of the juice remaining in the cooker. Broil, 6 inches from the heat source, for about 3 minutes, until the topping is browned. Serve hot.

Notes: *To roast and peel bell peppers, set them directly on top of a gas flame on the stovetop and cook, turning frequently, until softened and charred on the outside. Place them in a large bowl, cover with plastic wrap, and set aside until cool enough to handle. Slip the peel off with your fingers, leaving some of the blackened bits on the peppers. Cut in half and pull out the seeds and membranes and trim off the stem.*

You can assemble the tian in the baking dish up to 1 day in advance: Let it cool to room temperature, then cover and refrigerate. When ready to serve, top with the cheese and bread crumbs, then reheat the tian in a 375°F oven until bubbling and browned on top, about 10 minutes.

SOUTHERN-STYLE GREEN BEANS

Serves 4 to 6
4-quart slow cooker

2   pounds green beans, topped
    and tailed
½   onion, diced
1   smoked ham hock
    Salt and freshly ground
    black pepper

Southern *meaning they're cooked with smoked pork, and to oblivion, so they're buttery-tender.*

Cut the beans into 1-inch lengths and place them in a 4-quart slow cooker, along with the onion and ham hock. Add just enough water to barely cover the ingredients, stir in 1 teaspoon salt, then cook, covered, on the low setting for 8 to 10 hours, until the beans are extremely soft and can only generously be described as green. Remove the ham hock and pull off the meat, discarding the bone and fat. Return the meat to the cooker. Season well with salt and pepper to taste and serve hot.

SWEET & SOUR RED CABBAGE

Serves 4 to 6
6-quart slow cooker

1 cup cider vinegar
½ cup brown sugar
  Salt and freshly ground
  black pepper
1 teaspoon caraway seeds
  (optional)
1 large head red cabbage
  (about 3 pounds)
2 red apples (optional)

This is an extremely simple but homey and satisfying side dish. The apples will break down and meld with the liquids, thickening and enriching the dish, but the cabbage is good on its own as well.

In a 6-quart slow cooker, combine the vinegar, brown sugar, 1 teaspoon salt, the caraway (if using) and ½ cup water.

Peel off and discard the dried outer leaves of the cabbage. Cut the cabbage into quarters, then cut out and discard the core. Slice the cabbage into ½-inch strips and add them to the cooker. Core the apples (if using); cut them into thin slices and add to the cooker. Toss to combine all the ingredients. Cook, covered, on the low setting for 5 to 6 hours, until the cabbage is tender. Season to taste with salt and pepper and serve hot.

WILD RICE WITH CHERRIES & ORANGE

Serves 4 to 6
4-quart slow cooker

1½ cups wild rice

4   cups chicken or vegetable stock

1   orange
    Salt and freshly ground
    black pepper

½   cup dried cherries

2   tablespoons butter, cut
    into pieces

Wild rice takes forever to cook on the stovetop, and I just don't have the energy to keep checking to make sure the water isn't boiling over. Since it's going to take a long time anyway, you might as well just toss the rice in a slow cooker so you don't have to tend to it.

Put the rice and stock in a 4-quart slow cooker. Remove the zest of half of the orange with a vegetable peeler and add the strips of zest to the cooker. Season the stock with salt and pepper to taste. Cook, covered, on the low setting for 3 hours, or until the rice splits open and is tender but still chewy.

Add the cherries and cook for 10 minutes, until just softened, then drain the rice mixture in a sieve. Remove the cooked orange zest and discard. Grate the remaining orange zest and fold it into the rice, along with the butter. Taste and season again with salt and pepper if necessary, then transfer the rice to a serving bowl. Cut the white pith from the orange, cut the orange into segments, and arrange the pieces over the rice. Serve warm.

Pictured with Cassoulet on page 74

BRAISED BUTTERED ARTICHOKES & CELERY ROOT

Serves 4
4-quart slow cooker

4   large artichokes, or
     8 baby artichokes

½   lemon

4   ribs celery, leaves reserved

1   celery root (about 1¼ pounds)

4   tablespoons butter,
     cut into pieces
     Salt and freshly ground
     black pepper

2   thin slices pancetta, diced

Trim the tops off the artichokes and pull all the dark green leaves off to reveal the pale, tender leaves at the center. Cut the artichokes into quarters and scrape out the hairy, spiny choke in the centers. As you work, put the cut artichoke hearts in a bowl of water with the lemon half so they do not turn brown.

Slice the celery on the diagonal into ½-inch pieces. Peel the celery root and cut it into quarters, then slice the quarters into ½-inch pieces. Put the celery, celery root, and artichokes in a 4-quart slow cooker. Toss with the butter, 1 teaspoon salt, and ½ teaspoon pepper. Pour in ½ cup water, squeeze the lemon over the vegetables, and drop the lemon into the cooker. Cook, covered, on the low setting for 4 to 6 hours, until all the vegetables are very tender. Season to taste with salt and pepper and stir in the celery leaves. Cover the pot again and continue to cook for 20 minutes longer.

Meanwhile, in a small sauté pan or skillet over medium-high heat, cook the pancetta, stirring occasionally, until it's browned and crisp, about 4 minutes. Remove the pancetta to paper towels to drain.

Spoon the braised vegetables into a serving bowl and sprinkle with the pancetta. Serve hot.

MAQUE CHOUX

Serves 8
4-quart slow cooker

6 ears sweet corn, shucked, silk removed
1 small red bell pepper
1 small green bell pepper
½ medium onion
1 tomato (optional)
½ teaspoon cayenne pepper
   Salt and freshly ground black pepper
2 tablespoons butter, cut into pieces
½ cup heavy cream

Maque choux is a country Cajun dish that's usually cooked in a large Dutch oven on the stovetop and stirred and stirred to break up the corn and thicken its juices.

Cut the kernels from the corn cobs and put the corn and its juices in a 4-quart slow cooker. Seed and dice the bell peppers, dice the onion and the tomato, if using, and add the vegetables to the corn. Stir in the cayenne, 1 teaspoon salt, ½ teaspoon pepper, the butter, and ½ cup water. Cook, covered, on the low setting for 6 to 8 hours, until all the vegetables are tender.

Vigorously stir in the cream and cook on the high setting, uncovered, until heated through. Season to taste with more salt and pepper, if necessary. Serve hot.

PALAK PANEER

Serves 6
4-quart slow cooker

4 (10-ounce) boxes frozen chopped spinach, partially thawed

4 fresh hot green or red chiles such as serrano

1 3-inch piece fresh ginger, peeled and roughly chopped

1 cup whey from making Homemade Paneer (recipe follows), or water

1 tablespoon ground coriander

2 teaspoons ground cumin

1 teaspoon ground turmeric

½ teaspoon ground ginger

1 teaspoon paprika

½ teaspoon freshly ground black pepper

½ teaspoon sugar

4 tablespoons Ghee (page 50; see Notes)

6 whole dried red chiles such as arbol, stems removed
   Salt

3 ounces cream cheese

10 ounces Homemade Paneer (recipe follows; see Notes), cut into ¾-inch cubes

4 cloves garlic, thinly sliced

I have to admit that I never really liked this spinach and cheese dish, ubiquitous in Indian restaurants in New York. But then I trudged out to Sunnyside, Queens, to try a little restaurant called Mina, which I'd been reading about on Chowhound.com. Their palak paneer was absolutely transcendent, unlike any version of the dish I'd had before. Big, well-browned cubes of obviously fresh paneer, a texture like fluff, and the strange back-of-the-throat spiciness of lots of fresh ginger. It was also a little sweet, and the chef, Mina, had topped this particular bowl with fried garlic and maybe, if memory serves, a tangle of slowly caramelized shallot slivers. I've never been able to replicate Mina's palak paneer exactly, on the stovetop or in a slow cooker, but this version comes pretty close. Serve small portions, with an Indian flatbread such as naan, roti, or poori.

Put the spinach in a 4-quart slow cooker, breaking up the blocks a bit to nestle them tightly in the bottom of the cooker.

In a mini food processor or a blender, combine the fresh chiles, fresh ginger, ½ cup of the whey, the coriander, cumin, turmeric, ground ginger, paprika, pepper, and sugar. Process to a very fine puree. Heat 2 tablespoons of the ghee in a medium sauté pan over medium-high heat and add the spice puree. Cook, stirring, for 2 minutes. Scrape the mixture into the slow cooker over the spinach. Heat the remaining ½ cup whey in the pan and pour it over the spinach. Add the dried chiles and 2 teaspoons salt and cook, covered, on the low setting for 3 to 4 hours, pushing the spinach down and stirring once at some point after it has thawed. Stir in the cream cheese and continue to cook, uncovered, on the high setting, for about 20 minutes. Taste and add more salt if necessary.

Meanwhile, in a nonstick or very well seasoned sauté pan over medium-high heat, heat the remaining 2 tablespoons ghee. Carefully add the paneer cubes. Cook, without moving the pieces, for about 3 minutes, until well browned and crisp on the bottom, then use a spatula or tongs to turn the cubes over to cook one more side for 3 minutes. Transfer the browned paneer to the spinach in the slow cooker, leaving the ghee in the sauté pan. Gently fold the paneer cubes into the spinach mixture.

To the ghee in the sauté pan, add the garlic and cook over medium heat, stirring constantly, until golden brown.

Spoon the palak paneer onto individual serving plates or into small bowls and top with the browned garlic. Serve immediately.

Notes: Ghee is slow-cooked clarified butter, and is available in Indian markets and in specialty food stores; it's easy to make your own in a slow cooker (see page 50), but in a pinch you can just use clarified butter.

Paneer is a fresh cheese that's available in Southeast Asian markets. I much prefer to make it fresh, as the whey by-product adds a sweet-sour note to palak paneer.

Homemade Paneer

Makes about 10 ounces

½ gallon whole milk
⅓ cup strained fresh lemon juice

Line a fine-mesh sieve with three layers of rinsed and squeezed cheesecloth, with plenty of cheesecloth hanging over the edges. Place the sieve over a large bowl and set aside.

In a very clean, large pot, heat the milk over medium-high heat, stirring frequently with a clean spoon (if the milk starts to brown on the bottom of the pot, take care not to scrape up the browned bits with the spoon). When the milk reaches a full boil and foams almost all the way up to the top of the pot, remove from the heat and immediately drizzle in the lemon juice. Stir slowly, off the heat, for about 2 minutes, until white curds form and separate from the yellowish, clear whey. Slowly pour the mixture into the cheesecloth-lined sieve. Gather up the curds in the cheesecloth and twist the ends of the cloth together at the top. Rinse the wrapped ball of curds under warm running water, then return the ball to the sieve and press it into a disk shape. Weight it down with a can (a large can of tomatoes works well) and refrigerate for about 2 hours, until the cheese is firm and solid. Unwrap the disk of cheese and use it within 2 days.

HOT POLENTA WITH QUICK-ROASTED MUSHROOMS

Serves 4
4-quart slow cooker

For the polenta:

2 cups coarse-ground yellow
  cornmeal
1 tablespoon salt
3 tablespoons butter
¼ cup freshly grated Parmesan
  cheese

For the mushrooms:

½ pound mushrooms (such as
  shiitakes and chanterelles),
  wiped clean, tough stems
  removed
4 sprigs fresh thyme
3 cloves garlic, minced
1 tablespoon extra-virgin
  olive oil
1 tablespoon butter, or ghee
  foam and solids mixture
  (see page 50)
  Coarse sea salt
  Freshly ground black pepper

For serving:

2 cups mascarpone, chilled

This dish is all about the contrast between the cold, creamy mascarpone and the steaming-hot soft polenta that covers it.

Make the polenta: In a 4-quart slow cooker, combine the cornmeal, salt, and 6½ cups cold water. Cook, covered, on the low setting for 3 hours, or until thick. If you can, stir the polenta once or twice as it cooks. Stir in the butter and Parmesan and beat until smooth and uniform.

Make the mushrooms: Preheat the oven on the broiler setting or to 550°F. Cut the mushrooms into bite-size pieces (shiitakes into quarters, chanterelles in half). Strip the leaves off the thyme sprigs. In a medium ovenproof skillet over high heat, combine the oil and butter and heat until the butter is melted. Quickly add the mushrooms, thyme, garlic, and sea salt and pepper to taste, toss to combine, then immediately transfer the skillet to the oven. Roast for 5 minutes, or until the mushrooms are crisp at the edges and the garlic is golden brown.

In the middle of each of 4 individual serving plates, spoon ½ cup of the mascarpone. Top with hot polenta, then roasted mushrooms. Serve immediately.

ALL-DAY MARINARA SAUCE

Makes about 3 pints
6- to 7-quart slow cooker

4   (28-ounce) cans whole peeled
    Italian tomatoes
3   tablespoons olive oil
1   onion, finely diced
5   cloves garlic, minced
    Salt
3   large sprigs basil, plus ⅓ cup
    chopped or torn basil leaves
¾   teaspoon dried oregano
    Freshly ground black pepper
    Sugar or ¼ teaspoon baking
    soda (if necessary)

The slow cooker is the ideal vessel for long, slow marinara sauce. You don't have to watch it on the stove to keep it from boiling too hard, nor do you have to stir it to keep it from burning on the bottom of the pot. Just throw everything in and leave it alone until you're ready to use the sauce—with plain pasta, in lasagna, even on pizzas (if you like cooked sauce on pizzas)—or preserve it in jars to use later.

If you'd like to use fresh plum tomatoes instead of canned, drop them into boiling water for a couple of minutes, then slip the skins off and chop them in the blender as in the recipe. You'll need to cook fresh tomatoes longer, 8 to 10 hours on the low setting.

In a blender or food processor, roughly puree the tomatoes with their juices. (If the tomatoes are packed in puree rather than juice, you might need to add a little water to the sauce to thin it out a bit.) Put them in a 6- to 7-quart slow cooker.

In a sauté pan over medium-high heat, heat the oil, then add the onion and garlic and season lightly with salt. Cook, stirring frequently, until the onion starts to become translucent, about 4 minutes. Scrape the mixture into the cooker. Add the basil sprigs, oregano, 1 teaspoon salt, and ½ teaspoon pepper. Cook, covered, on the low setting for 6 to 8 hours. If the sauce is too thin after 6 hours, cook on the high setting with the lid on sideways for 1 hour, or until thickened to your liking. Remove and discard the cooked basil. Stir in the chopped basil, season again with salt and pepper, and add a bit of sugar or the baking soda if the sauce is too acidic. Serve immediately, or can the sauce for future use, or freeze it in small containers for up to several months.

GHEE

Makes about 5 cups
4-quart slow cooker

3   pounds unsalted butter

This could well be one of the best uses for the slow cooker. The low, even heat required for making ghee is difficult to maintain on a stovetop or even in the oven without near-constant attention, but in a slow cooker it's perfectly foolproof.

Don't be tempted to cook more than three pounds of butter in a 4-quart slow cooker, as the butter sometimes pops and bubbles several inches above the surface of the liquid. If you want to make a larger batch, use a larger cooker, and don't fill it more than halfway with butter.

Cut the butter into large (½-stick) chunks and place them in a 4-quart slow cooker. Cook, uncovered or with the lid on sideways, on the high setting for 4 to 5 hours, until a dry-looking layer of foam forms on the surface and the solids that settle at the bottom are caramel-colored rather than white—the foam will be just starting to brown at the edge of the cooker insert. Do not stir the butter or disturb the cooker as the butter cooks (if the solids are jostled, the butter will bubble up and pop furiously; if this happens, set the lid over the cooker until the bubbling subsides).

When the butter has stopped bubbling, use a large flat spoon to skim off the foam, putting the foam in a small container. Carefully, slowly, ladle the clear golden liquid through a very fine-mesh sieve (or a sieve lined with three layers of cheesecloth) into clean glass jars, taking care not to disturb the solids on the side and bottom of the cooker insert. Stop ladling well before you reach the solids on the bottom. Let the ghee cool to room temperature, then put the lids on the jars and store in a cool place or in the refrigerator for up to several months.

Pour the remaining liquid and the solids at the bottom into the small container with the foam, and stir to combine—this can be refrigerated for up to 1 week (see Don't Discard the Foam).

Don't Discard the Foam
The foam-solids mixture that is a by-product of making ghee is itself almost reason to throw three pounds of butter into the slow cooker. I like it spread on a baguette, with just a thin slice of ham or a slice of havarti and one of sweet crisp apple. It can also be used instead of butter on vegetables and for sautéing (although watch it carefully, as it will brown quickly)—try it in the quick-roasted mushrooms in the recipe on page 48.

DAL

Serves 4
4-quart slow cooker

½ head cauliflower, broken into florets

1 large parsnip, peeled and cut into ½-inch pieces

1 Granny Smith apple, peeled, cored, and cut into ½-inch pieces

½ small onion, diced

1 1-inch piece fresh ginger, peeled and minced

½ cup brown lentils, picked over and rinsed

½ cup yellow split peas, picked over and rinsed

½ cup wheatberries, picked over and rinsed

½ cup hulled barley, picked over and rinsed

1 teaspoon ground cumin

1 teaspoon ground coriander

½ teaspoon ground turmeric

2 dried hot red chiles; or 1 fresh hot chile, minced (optional)

Salt

Juice of 1 lemon

¼ cup chopped fresh cilantro

1 tablespoon Ghee (page 50)

1½ teaspoons cumin seeds

1½ teaspoons black mustard seeds

4 sprigs fresh cilantro, for garnish

This beautiful, almost ridiculously healthful dal is a riot of textures: The split peas break down as they cook, while the wheatberries and barley stay firm, and the quickly fried whole mustard and cumin seeds (a common last-minute addition to dals) have a fun crisp pop to them. Feel free to substitute other vegetables for the cauliflower, parsnip, and apple (though I love the light colors and the hint of sweetness in this combination), and of course you needn't use all of the pulses and grains listed here—just use about 2 cups total, and use at least one pulse (to yield a creamy, thick soup) and one grain (for nutty chewiness).

Put the cauliflower, parsnip, apple, onion, ginger, lentils, split peas, wheatberries, barley, ground cumin, coriander, turmeric, and the chiles (if using) in a 4-quart slow cooker. Add 5 cups water and cook, covered, on the low setting for 6 to 7 hours, until the pulses and grains are soft and the vegetables are just beginning to break down. Season generously with salt to taste and stir in the lemon juice and chopped cilantro.

In a small saucepan over medium-high heat, melt the ghee. Add the cumin seeds and mustard seeds—they will sputter and pop almost immediately—and cook, stirring, for about 20 seconds, then scrape the spices and ghee into the slow cooker and stir to combine. Remove and discard the dried chiles, if used. Serve the dal hot, garnished with the cilantro sprigs.

LIGHTER FARE

BUTTERNUT SQUASH SOUP

Serves 4
4-quart slow cooker

1   large butternut squash (about
    2 pounds)
1   tablespoon butter
1   cinnamon stick
    Pinch of freshly grated nutmeg
1   teaspoon sugar (optional)
    Salt and freshly ground
    black pepper
4   sprigs fresh thyme, plus more
    for garnish
1   tablespoon sweet sherry
    (oloroso optional)
2   medium shallots
1   tablespoon extra-virgin
    olive oil
2   tablespoons heavy cream

Peel the squash and cut it in half lengthwise. Scoop out the seeds and stringy centers, then cut the flesh into 1-inch chunks. Place in a 4-quart slow cooker and pour in 2 cups water. Add the butter, cinnamon, nutmeg, sugar, 2 teaspoons salt, and $\frac{1}{2}$ teaspoon pepper. Cook, covered, on the low setting for about 6 hours, until the squash is very soft. Strip the leaves from the thyme sprigs and add them to the soup. Remove and discard the cinnamon. Using an immersion (stick) blender, puree the soup until smooth. (Alternatively, transfer the squash and liquid to a regular blender and puree, then return it to the cooker.) Stir in the sherry, if using. Continue to cook on the low setting for 10 minutes.

Meanwhile, peel and thinly slice the shallots. In a small sauté pan, heat the oil over medium heat. Add the shallots and cook, stirring constantly, until the shallots are golden brown but not burned, about 3 minutes. Using a slotted spoon, transfer the shallots to paper towels to drain. Stir the oil into the soup and season with salt and pepper to taste.

Ladle the soup into 4 wide, shallow serving bowls. Drizzle $\frac{1}{2}$ tablespoon of the cream over each serving and garnish with the fried shallots and thyme sprigs. Serve immediately.

Pictured on page 52

EASIEST CORN CHOWDER

Serves 4 to 6
4-quart slow cooker

½ onion, diced

2 carrots, diced

3 interior ribs celery, diced,
   leaves reserved

2 russet potatoes, peeled
   and diced

3 cups sweet corn kernels
   (cut off 4 cobs, or frozen)

1 bay leaf
   Salt and freshly ground
   black pepper

1 tablespoon flour

¼ cup heavy cream

¼ cup chopped fresh flat-leaf
   parsley

If you have a craving for corn chowder that's been brewing all winter, spring, and early summer, this will satisfy it. If you've been eating corn chowder all July and August and are ready for a slightly more involved—and more soulful—version that will hold you over till next summer, see Mmm…Bacon below.

Put the onion, carrots, celery, potatoes, corn, and bay leaf in a 4-quart slow cooker. Sprinkle with 1 teaspoon salt and 1 teaspoon pepper, then pour in 2½ cups water. Cook, covered, on the low setting for 4 to 5 hours, until the vegetables are soft.

Ladle some of the liquid into a small cup and add the flour to the cup, stirring until smooth. Pour the slurry back into the soup and stir to combine; cook on the high setting for 30 minutes, or until thickened slightly.

Mince the celery leaves. Stir in the cream, along with the parsley and celery leaves. Taste and add more salt and pepper if necessary. Serve hot.

Mmm…Bacon
If you like, begin the chowder by cooking 8 slices bacon in a large deep skillet or pot over medium heat until crisp. Remove the bacon to paper towels to drain; crumble and set aside. Pour off all but 1 tablespoon of the bacon fat and return the skillet to medium-high heat. Add the onion, carrots, and celery, then sprinkle the vegetables with the flour. Cook, stirring, until the flour is beginning to turn golden brown. Add 2½ cups water and stir to loosen any browned bits on the bottom of the pan; pour the vegetables and liquid into the slow cooker. Add the potatoes, corn, bay leaf, and salt and pepper to taste and cook on the low setting for 4 to 5 hours. Stir in the cream, parsley, and celery leaves, season again, and serve sprinkled with the bacon.

WHITE BEAN & KALE SOUP WITH ROSEMARY OIL

Serves 6
4-quart slow cooker

12 ounces dried cannellini beans
    (1½ cups)
½   pound smoked pork neck
    bone, or 1 smoked ham hock
    (optional; see Note)
1   medium onion, coarsely
    chopped
2   large cloves garlic, coarsely
    chopped
1   bay leaf
1   bunch kale (about 1 pound),
    rinsed, stemmed, and torn
    into 2-inch pieces
    Salt and freshly ground
    black pepper
3   tablespoons extra-virgin
    olive oil
6   sprigs fresh rosemary

Rinse the beans under cold running water and pick through them, removing any stones or debris. Place the beans, pork neck bone, onion, garlic, bay leaf, and 5 cups water in a 4-quart slow cooker. Cook, covered, on the low setting for 4 hours.

Using tongs, remove the pork from the cooker and set it aside. Add the kale to the cooker, pushing it down into the liquid, replace the lid, and cook for 1 hour longer, or until the kale is very tender. When the pork is cool enough to handle, pull the meat off the bones, discarding the bones and fat. Return the meat to the cooker, season with salt and pepper to taste, and cook to heat through.

In a medium skillet over medium-high heat, heat the oil until hot but not smoking. Add the rosemary sprigs and fry, turning them with tongs, for 1 to 2 minutes, until just starting to brown. Remove the rosemary from the oil and set it aside on paper towels to drain and become crisp. Set the oil aside.

Ladle the soup into 6 serving bowls and drizzle each serving with some of the rosemary-infused oil. Place a fried rosemary sprig on top of each serving.

Note: The meat is used here mainly as a seasoning (and can be omitted if you'd like to make a vegetarian version of this soup—the rosemary adds so much flavor that you won't miss the meat). For a more substantial dish, instead of the neck bone (or in addition to it) use 1 pound smoked sausage, such as kielbasa or andouille, sliced on the diagonal into 1-inch pieces.

HOT AND SOUR SOUP

Serves 4 to 6

6   cups Basic Chicken or Vegetable Stock (page 58)

8   dried shiitake mushroom caps, or 1 cup dried wood ear mushrooms

⅓   cup white or rice vinegar

4   tablespoons soy sauce

2   tablespoons hot chile oil

1   tablespoon chile-garlic paste

1   teaspoon sugar

1   cup julienned sliced cooked bamboo shoots (one 8-ounce can)

1   large egg, lightly beaten

1   cooked chicken breast, boned and shredded (optional)

6   ounces firm bean curd ("tofu," if it's not in Asian food), pressed for at least 30 minutes underneath a heavy weight

2   scallions

Every once in a while, when I was in high school, my friends Lennaya and Clover and I would splurge on Chinese food in the big town of Leesburg, Virginia, at a little storefront restaurant called the China King, which was, conveniently, just around the corner from the Tally-Ho movie theater in the old part of town. It had an aquarium in the front window that was sparsely populated by what seemed at the time to be very exotic tropical fish. I was devoted to the beef with tender ginger slices, and the old-school hot and sour soup. Since moving to New York, though, and discovering "real" Chinese food, the old hot and sour—when I've had the guts to order it here (how provincial)—has consistently let me down. So the other day, feeling nostalgic and thinking of my old friends and how far we've dispersed since the Tally-Ho days, I decided to try to make my own hot and sour soup. As it turns out, this is much, much better than anything I could ever hope to find in any Chinese restaurant, real or otherwise. Though lacking the gag-inducing viscosity of the traditional cornstarch thickened broth and the lockjaw effect of excessive amounts of MSG, this soup, truly hot and truly sour, with the fresh crunch of bamboo shoots and the creamy nuttiness of bean curd, may well bring back memories of your own first but not last bowl.

If using shiitake mushrooms, heat 1 cup of the stock in a saucepan to boiling and add the mushrooms; let soak for 10 minutes, then drain, reserving the soaking liquid, and slice the shiitakes into ¼-inch slivers. (If using dried wood ear mushrooms, there's no need to presoak or slice them.)

Put the remaining stock, the soaking liquid, mushrooms, vinegar, soy sauce, chile oil, chile-garlic paste, sugar, and bamboo shoots in a 4-quart slow cooker. Cook, covered, on the low setting for about 6 hours, or until the mushrooms and bamboo shoots are quite soft and the flavors have melded. Turn the cooker to high, and when the soup is bubbling around the edge of the pot, lift the lid and gradually pour in the egg, whisking with a fork to break up the egg as it cooks in the soup. Stir in the chicken and bean curd, cover the cooker, and cook until heated through, about 20 minutes. Dice the bean curd and thinly slice the scallions.

Ladle the soup into deep serving bowls and sprinkle the scallions over the top. Serve immediately. (This soup keeps well, tightly covered, in the refrigerator for several days.)

BASIC CHICKEN OR VEGETABLE STOCK

Makes about 3 quarts

1   large carrot
½   onion
2   ribs celery, with leaves
1   bunch parsley stems
1   bay leaf
1   teaspoon whole black
     peppercorns
½ to 1 pound raw chicken
     trimmings, such as backs,
     necks, wing tips, and other
     bones (optional)

If you're roasting a chicken for dinner, first cut out the backbone and chop off the wing tips (the best way to roast chicken anyway is to remove the backbone and open the body out flat on top of a bunch of lemon slices); throw them in a heavy-duty resealable plastic bag and store them in the freezer. When you have about a pound of trimmings, put them in the slow cooker (frozen is fine as long as they're smallish pieces so they'll thaw quickly) with vegetables and aromatics and some water; go out and take in a double bill (or go to work), and you'll have a good basic stock ready to use in a quick soup when you come home— you probably won't even have to skim any foam off the top, and you can leave the fat in the stock if time is short, as there won't be terribly much of it. Or forget the chicken altogether and just make an easy nonfat vegetable stock.

Roughly chop the carrot, onion, and celery and add them, along with the remaining ingredients, including the chicken trimmings (if using) to a 4-quart slow cooker. Fill the cooker three quarters full with cold water. Cook, covered, on the low setting for 6 to 8 hours, until the stock is yellow and flavorful. If there is any foam on the surface of the stock, skim it off and discard. Carefully pour the stock through a fine-mesh sieve into a large bowl and discard the solids.

Let the stock cool to room temperature, then chill in the refrigerator. Skim the fat from the surface of the chilled stock, then pour the clear yellow liquid into a separate container, leaving behind and discarding any solids at the bottom of the bowl. Use the stock within a few days, or put it in a tightly sealed plastic container and freeze for up to six months.

LINGUINE WITH DUCK CONFIT & MUSHROOMS

Serves 2

Salt

½ pound dried linguine

1 tablespoon duck or goose fat

1 medium red onion, cut vertically into ¼-inch slices

2 portobello mushrooms, caps and stems sliced ¼ inch thick

1 cup meat from 2 legs Duck Confit (page 21)

1 teaspoon fresh thyme leaves

2 tablespoons chopped fresh flat-leaf parsley

¼ cup heavy cream

Freshly ground black pepper

Fresh thyme or parsley sprigs

This is a great way to use slow-cooked confit—a quick pasta sauce in which the meat is paired with earthy mushrooms, a classic combination.

In a large pot of boiling salted water, cook the pasta until just *al dente*.

Meanwhile, in a large sauté pan over high heat, heat the duck fat. Add the onion and mushrooms and cook, stirring frequently, until the onion is soft and the mushrooms are well browned, about 6 minutes. Add the duck meat and cook until just starting to brown, about 3 minutes, then add the thyme leaves, parsley, cream, and salt and pepper to taste. Ladle about ¼ cup of the pasta cooking water into the pan. Cook until the sauce has thickened slightly and everything is just heated through, about 4 minutes.

Drain the pasta and add it to the pan. Toss to coat the pasta with the sauce, then divide it between 2 serving plates. Garnish with the thyme sprigs and serve immediately.

RED RISOTTO

Serves 4
4-quart slow cooker

2   red onions
2   cloves garlic
2   tablespoons olive oil
2   cups Arborio (short-grain) rice
1   cup red wine
4 to 5 cups vegetable stock or
      water, or a combination
      Salt and freshly ground
      black pepper
½   large head radicchio, or
      1 small head
2   ounces freshly grated
      Parmesan cheese, plus more
      for serving
2   tablespoons butter (optional)

My friend and one-time downstairs neighbor, Liza, served something like this risotto at a Valentine's Day dinner party. I never got her recipe, but when I later spent a month living in Italy I found myself making this nearly every day, simply because I couldn't resist the deep-red, bitter Treviso radicchio being hawked in the markets every morning. It's certainly easy enough to make in a conventional sauté pan on the stovetop—it takes about 45 minutes of frequent stirring. But if you want to be able to concentrate on other things instead of stirring the risotto, the slow cooker's the way to go.

Slice the onions lengthwise into ½-inch slivers, and roughly chop the garlic. In a large sauté pan, heat 1 tablespoon of the oil and add the onions and garlic; cook over medium-high heat until the onions are slightly softened, about 5 minutes. Scrape the mixture into a 4-quart slow cooker.

Return the pan to medium-high heat and add the remaining 1 tablespoon oil and the rice. Cook, stirring, for 3 to 4 minutes, until the rice is hot and completely coated with the oil. Pour in the wine and cook for 1 minute, stirring, until most of the wine has been absorbed by the rice or has evaporated. Scrape the rice into the cooker. Add 4 cups of the stock, 1 teaspoon salt, and ½ teaspoon pepper and stir to combine. Cook, covered, on the high setting for about 2 hours, until the rice is tender but still *al dente* and the mixture is creamy and thick but still quite liquidy. If necessary, heat up more stock or water in a saucepan and add up to 1 cup more stock to the rice.

Core the radicchio and slice it into ½-inch ribbons. Fold the radicchio and cheese into the rice, cover the cooker, and continue to cook for 20 minutes longer, until the radicchio is wilted and softened and the cheese is melted. Stir in the butter, if using. Taste and season with more salt and pepper, if necessary. Serve hot, sprinkled with a little more cheese.

POSOLE ROJO

Serves 6 to 8
4-quart slow cooker

2½ pounds pork spare ribs,
   trimmed of excess fat

8 cloves garlic, peeled

1 teaspoon dried epazote leaves
   (available in Latino markets;
   optional)

½ teaspoon dried oregano,
   preferably Mexican

4 cups chicken stock or water

6 dried guajillo chiles, stems
   and seeds removed

6 dried mulato chiles, stems
   and seeds removed

1 small onion, roughly chopped

2 (15-ounce) cans hominy,
   drained and rinsed
   Salt
   Juice of 1 lime

Toppings:
   Fried corn tortilla strips
   tossed with salt
   Thinly sliced radishes
   Sprigs of fresh cilantro
   Sliced avocado
   Lime wedges

If you'd prefer to use dried hominy instead of canned, add 1½ cups (about 10 ounces) to the slow cooker right at the beginning of the cooking time, on top of the pork, and add 1 cup water when you add the stock. The hominy will be slightly softer and will break apart a bit more than if you use canned, making the stew thicker.

Put the pork in a 4-quart slow cooker and add 6 cloves of the garlic, the epazote (if using), and oregano. Pour in the stock and cook on the low setting, covered, for 6 hours, or until the meat is falling off the bones.

Meanwhile, pour 3 cups boiling water over the chiles and let them soak for 30 minutes. Place the chiles and soaking liquid in a blender, along with the remaining 2 cloves garlic and the onion, and puree. Set aside.

Using tongs, remove and discard the bones and fat from the pork ribs. Pour the chile puree into the cooker, stir in the hominy, and continue to cook, covered, for 30 minutes longer, until heated through. Season generously with salt to taste and stir in the lime juice. Ladle the posole into wide, shallow soup plates and serve with the toppings in separate small bowls alongside.

HEARTY STEWS

VENISON & APPLE KORESH

Serves 4
4-quart slow cooker

1   tablespoon vegetable oil

2   pounds venison stew meat,
    (shoulder or leg) cut into
    large bite-size cubes

1   onion, chopped

1   teaspoon salt

½   teaspoon freshly ground
    black pepper

½   teaspoon ground cinnamon

½   cup yellow split peas

1   tablespoon tomato paste

3   tablespoons sugar

3   tablespoons cider vinegar

½   teaspoon saffron threads in
    2 tablespoons boiling water

3   apples

1   tablespoon butter

Shalah Williams, an Iranian who's lived in deer-plagued northern Virginia for many years, taught my mom how to make this tangy, slightly sweet koresh, a stew that is usually identified by the fruit that is featured ("apple koresh," "apricot koresh") rather than the meat, which is generally lamb. You can use lamb- or beef-stew meat instead of venison.

In a large skillet or sauté pan, heat the oil over medium-high heat. Add the venison and cook until nicely browned, about 8 minutes. Transfer the meat to a 4-quart slow cooker. Add all the remaining ingredients except the apples and butter and pour in 2 cups water. Cook, covered, on the low setting for 6 hours.

Peel and core the apples and cut them into large chunks. Heat the butter in a large skillet over high heat. Add the apples and cook until lightly browned, about 8 minutes.

Turn the slow cooker to the high setting and fold in the apples. Cook, uncovered, for 1 hour, or until the apples are tender and the sauce is thickened somewhat. Serve hot.

Pictured on page 64

BEEF & SWEET POTATO STEW WITH GROUND TOASTED RICE

Serves 4
6- to 7-quart slow cooker

1½ pounds beef stew meat, such as chuck, in 1½- to 2-inch chunks)

Salt and freshly ground black pepper

1 teaspoon vegetable oil

1 teaspoon ground cinnamon

½ teaspoon ground cumin

¼ teaspoon ground ginger

¼ teaspoon cayenne pepper

3 medium sweet potatoes, peeled and cut into 2-inch chunks

2 small onions, sliced

2 cloves garlic, sliced

¼ cup basmati rice

½ cup unsalted peanuts

⅓ cup dried apricots (optional)

¼ pound green beans, trimmed

½ cup chopped cilantro leaves

It seems that every slow-cooker cookbook has to have a recipe for a beef-and-green-beans dish, with protein, green vegetable, and starch all in one pot. This is my take on it, a hybrid of the classic Filipino stew kari-kari, which is thickened with ground toasted rice (try this to thicken other stews that might emerge from the slow cooker a bit watery), and a West African beef-and-yam dish with peanuts (or groundnuts).

Season the beef with salt and pepper. In a large skillet or sauté pan, heat the oil over medium-high heat. Add the beef and cook, turning frequently, until browned on all sides, about 8 minutes. Transfer to a 6- to 7-quart slow cooker and season with the cinnamon, cumin, ginger, and cayenne.

Return the skillet to high heat and pour in 1½ cups water, scraping up any browned bits on the bottom of the pan. Bring to a boil, then pour the water over the beef in the cooker. Layer on the sweet potatoes, onions, and garlic. Cook, covered, on the low setting for 2½ to 3 hours, until the beef is tender and the sweet potatoes are soft but still hold their shape.

Meanwhile, in a small skillet over medium heat, toast the rice, shaking and stirring constantly, until evenly browned, about 4 minutes. Transfer the rice to a plate to cool, then grind to a powder in a spice mill (pass the powder through a sieve and discard the large pieces left in the sieve). Grind half of the peanuts and coarsely chop the other half.

Add the powdered rice and ground peanuts to the beef mixture and stir gently, taking care not to break up the sweet potatoes too much. Bring a small saucepan of salted water to a boil and drop in the apricots (if using) and the green beans. Boil for 4 to 5 minutes, until the beans are bright green and crisp-tender; drain and gently stir the apricots and beans into the stew. Season to taste with salt and pepper and serve in large bowls sprinkled with the chopped peanuts and cilantro.

TEXAS CHILI

Serves 4
4-quart slow cooker

12 dried ancho chiles

2 dried guajillo chiles

2 ounces suet, chopped (see Notes)

3 pounds beef round or lean chuck, cut into ½-inch cubes

2 cloves garlic, minced

1 bay leaf

1 teaspoon granulated garlic or garlic powder

½ teaspoon ground cumin (optional)

About 1½ cups beef broth

Salt and freshly ground black pepper

¼ cup *masa harina* (see Notes)

No beans, no tomatoes, no onions. Serve this purist's chili with cornbread, or hoe-cakes fried in bacon fat in a cast-iron skillet. And maybe a salad if you dare.

Snap the stems off the dried chiles and shake out the seeds; discard the stems and seeds. Put the chiles in a heatproof bowl and pour boiling water over them to just cover. Soak for 30 minutes.

In a large skillet, cook the suet over medium heat until all the fat is rendered (melted) and only small pieces of solid gristle remain in the pan, about 5 minutes. Use a slotted spoon to remove and discard the solid pieces, then pour the fat into a 4-quart slow cooker.

In the same skillet over high heat, cook the beef, in three batches to avoid crowding the pan, until no longer pink on the outside; drain the beef in a colander, then add it to the cooker, along with the minced garlic, bay leaf, granulated garlic, and cumin, if using.

Place the chiles and their soaking liquid in a mini food processor or a blender and process to a fine puree. Pour the puree through a sieve into the cooker and discard the pieces of tough skin and stray seeds left in the sieve.

Add about 1 cup of the broth, to almost cover the beef in the cooker, and about 1 teaspoon salt and ½ teaspoon pepper, and stir to combine all the ingredients. Cook, covered, on the low setting for 4 to 5 hours, until the beef is tender.

In a small bowl or measuring cup, combine the remaining ½ cup broth with the *masa harina*. Pour the mixture into the stew and cook, covered, on the low setting, for another 30 minutes to 1 hour, until thickened. Season to taste with salt and pepper and serve hot.

Notes: Suet, the solid fat that surrounds beef kidneys, imparts a deep beef flavor to this determindly beefcentric chili, but you can substitute lard, vegetable shortening, or vegetable oil.

Masa Harina is lime-treated ground corn—the grain used to make corn tortillas and tamales. It can be found with the baking ingredients in most supermarkets.

Fresh Corn Hoecakes

Makes about 14

1   cup yellow cornmeal
1   cup all-purpose flour
2   tablespoons baking powder
1   teaspoon salt
2   large eggs
1   cup buttermilk
1   tablespoon melted bacon grease or butter, or vegetable oil, plus more for frying
1   cup fresh sweet corn kernels (cut from 1 large cob)

I'd never had a hoecake before moving to the big small town of Louisville, Kentucky, with my friend Derek—the one I'd marry three-plus years and a couple of states later. Way over on Dixie Highway (we didn't have a car, and it was too far to walk from First Street in that oppressively still, muggy heat, thick with oak pollen, peculiar to the Ohio River Valley)— there was this cruddy-looking pink-painted cinderblock barbecue place called—I swear—Pig Out. When my dad came to town to visit me (and, no doubt, to check out this Derek), he took us there in his car, and was so impressed with the fare that he insisted we order an extra slab of ribs and some hoecakes to take home with us for later. After that, whenever Derek and I had access to a vehicle not affiliated with the city bus system we'd go to Pig Out. It was always closed. I never had those hoecakes again.

In a medium bowl, whisk together the cornmeal, flour, baking powder, and salt. In a separate bowl, combine the eggs, buttermilk, 1/2 cup water, and the 1 tablespoon bacon grease. Pour the liquid ingredients into the dry ingredients and stir gently to just combine. Fold in the corn kernels and set the batter aside.

Heat 1 tablespoon bacon grease in a heavy skillet over medium high heat. Spoon 1/4-cup puddles of the batter into the skillet and cook for 2 minutes on the first side and about 1 minute on the second, or until nicely browned. Remove the hoecakes to a plate in a warm oven until all are cooked. Repeat with the remaining batter, adding more grease to the skillet as necessary. Serve hot.

CINCINNATI-STYLE CHILI

Serves 6
4-quart slow cooker

1   teaspoon whole allspice
1   teaspoon whole cloves
2   cinnamon sticks
1   bay leaf
2½ pounds finely ground lean
    beef such as sirloin (see Note)
1   (15-ounce) can crushed
    tomatoes
½   large onion, finely diced
4   cloves garlic, minced
1½ teaspoons ground cinnamon
1   teaspoon ground cumin
1   teaspoon cayenne pepper
1   tablespoon Worcestershire sauce
    Salt and freshly ground
    black pepper
1   pound dried spaghetti
1   (15-ounce) can red kidney
    beans, drained and rinsed
1   ounce unsweetened chocolate,
    chopped
8   ounces cheddar cheese,
    finely shredded

My husband, Derek, introduced me to Cincinnati chili when we lived in Louisville, which is as close as I've ever gotten to spending any time in Cincinnati proper. This chili, we both agreed, is spicier (and in my opinion therefore more interesting) than the Skyline chain's fast-food-ish version: If what you're after is strict authenticity, cut the cayenne in half, or use chile powder instead, and you'll come darn close. This is a four-way (spaghetti, beans, chili, cheese); for a five-way, pile finely diced raw onions between the beans and the chili. Serve with oyster crackers.

Tie the allspice, cloves, cinnamon sticks, and bay leaf together in a double layer of cheesecloth and place the bag in a 4-quart slow cooker.

In a large skillet, working in two batches if necessary, cook the beef over medium-high heat until no trace of pink remains, about 10 minutes. Drain off the fat, then add the beef to the slow cooker, along with the tomatoes, 1½ cups water, the onion, garlic, ground cinnamon, cumin, cayenne, Worcestershire sauce, 1 teaspoon salt, and ½ teaspoon pepper. Cook, covered, on the low setting for 6 hours.

When ready to serve, cook the pasta in a large pot of boiling water until *al dente*; drain well and set aside. Place the beans in a small saucepan with enough water to cover, and bring to a simmer. Cook until heated through, then drain.

Stir the chocolate into the chili until melted, then season with salt and pepper to taste. Remove and discard the bag of whole spices.

Divide the pasta among 6 serving plates, then top with a spoonful of beans, ladle chili over the beans, and top with a big mound of cheese.

Note: A very fine grind is essential here in order to achieve the correct texture: Use a meat grinder fitted with the plate with the smallest holes, or ask your butcher to grind it for you.

CASSOULET

Serves 6 to 8
6- to 7-quart slow cooker

1   pound dried small white beans, soaked overnight in cold water to cover by several inches

1   bouquet garni (1 bunch parsley stems, 1 bay leaf, and 1 sprig thyme, tied in cheesecloth)

1   small onion

6   cloves garlic

    About 3 tablespoons fat from Duck Confit (page 21)

1   large carrot

2   ribs celery

1   pound lamb stew meat (shoulder or leg), cut into 1-inch chunks

1   pound pork stew meat (shoulder), cut into 1-inch chunks

1   thick smoked pork chop

½   pound smoked sausage such as kielbasa

1   cup wine, red or white

1   cup beef stock or water

3   tablespoons tomato sauce or paste (optional)

    Salt and freshly ground pepper

This is an extremely rich and hearty winter stew of white beans and several kinds of meat, and the proportions I've given here result in an almost absurdly luxurious ratio of meat to beans. Feel free to use more beans and less meat, or to substitute other meats (fresh pork chops, spare ribs, ham, beef short ribs) for the ones I've suggested here: As long as there's pork in the pot, you're in good shape.

I've found that fresh sausages tend to lose some of their snappiness after a stint in the slow cooker, so here I've suggested cooking the sausages separately and adding them at the end. That said, it's perfectly acceptable to quickly brown the sausages when you brown the other meats and add them to the cooker at the beginning.

Drain the beans and put them in a 6- to 7-quart slow cooker. Cover them with water and add the bouquet garni.

Dice the onion and roughly chop the garlic. Heat 1 tablespoon of the duck fat in a large sauté pan over medium-high heat and add the onion and garlic; cook, stirring frequently, until the onion is wilted and just starting to become translucent, about 4 minutes. Scrape the onion and garlic into the cooker. Cut the carrot and celery into large chunks and add them to the cooker.

Return the sauté pan to medium-high heat. Working in batches, and adding more fat as necessary, brown the lamb, fresh pork, smoked pork and its bone, and the smoked sausage; add the meats to the cooker as they brown. To the sauté pan over high heat, add the wine, stirring to scrape up all the browned bits on the bottom of the pan. Boil the wine until it's thick and nearly evaporated, then pour in the stock; bring to a boil, then stir the liquid into the meats and beans in the cooker, along with the tomato sauce, if using.

Cook, covered, on the low setting for 6 to 8 hours, until the beans are soft but still hold their shape and the meats are tender. Skim off the foam and clear fat that rises to the surface; if the cassoulet is too liquidy (it should be the consistency of a thick stew), spoon off some of the juices. Taste and add salt and pepper as necessary.

6 to 8 small links (about 1 pound) Sweet-Spiced Sausage (recipe follows), or other garlicky, strongly spiced fresh sausage Meat from 2 legs Duck Confit (page 21), in large chunks, or goose confit

¼ cup chopped fresh flat-leaf parsley

2 tablespoons chopped celery leaves

When ready to serve, heat a sauté pan over medium heat, add some duck fat and the fresh sausage, and cook, turning occasionally, until nicely browned and just cooked through, about 12 minutes. Arrange the sausages over the meats and vegetables in the cooker. Return the saucepan to medium-high heat and add the duck confit. Cook, turning frequently, until browned and crisp on the outside and heated through, about 4 minutes. Add the duck to the cassoulet. Remove and discard the bouquet garni. Stir in the parsley and celery leaves and serve.

Croutons for Cassoulet
Cut thin slices of baguette, brush them lightly with fat from the duck confit, toast them, and set them atop the cassoulet right before serving.

SWEET-SPICED GARLIC SAUSAGE

Makes about 3 pounds,
or about 18 small links

3   pounds not-too-lean boneless
    pork shoulder meat,
    cut into chunks

6   cloves garlic, finely minced

2   teaspoons salt

1½ teaspoons ground cinnamon

½   teaspoon ground cloves

½   nutmeg, freshly grated

½   teaspoon cayenne pepper

½   teaspoon freshly ground
    black pepper

¼   cup sweet sherry (oloroso)
    About 5 feet hog casings,
    rinsed well inside
    and out (see Note)

Using a meat grinder fitted with the plate having medium-size holes, grind the pork. Combine the pork, garlic, salt, cinnamon, cloves, nutmeg, cayenne, black pepper, sherry, and ½ cup cold water. Set aside in the refrigerator while you prepare a sausage stuffer (take the grinding plate off the meat grinder and attach the sausage-stuffing tube, or put a sausage-stuffing attachment on a heavy-duty stand mixer).

Stuff the casings somewhat loosely with the pork mixture, twisting off links every few inches. Pat the sausages dry with paper towels and refrigerate, covered, until you are ready to cook them; alternatively, wrap them tightly and freeze for up to several months.

Note: You can buy hog casings (cleaned intestines) at some butcher shops—if they make their own sausages, they'll probably sell you the casings, too. The ones I get are packed in salt, and they keep "forever" in the refrigerator, according to the guy at Esposito Pork Shop. A small container of 45 feet of casings costs me about four dollars. Before using them, rinse them well in several changes of cold water, then put one end of the casing over the opening of the faucet and run cold water all the way through it to plump it up. Keep the casings in cold water while you're preparing the stuffing.

CAJUN RED BEANS & RICE

Serves 4 to 6
6- to 7-quart slow cooker

1   pound dried red kidney beans
1   pound spicy smoked pork
    sausage such as andouille
    or kielbasa
2   green bell peppers
2   ribs celery
1   large onion
3   cloves garlic
1   bay leaf
2   teaspoons flour (optional)
½ to 1 teaspoon cayenne pepper,
    to taste
    Salt and freshly ground
    black pepper
2   cups long-grain rice

On a road trip through the South a few years ago my companion and I were taken in for a weekend by an exceedingly generous Cajun named Mr. Albert. We slept over at his house in Church Point, Louisiana, and when we woke up the next morning our host had a pot of these red beans and sausage on the stove along with one of pot roast (see Spoon Beef, page 86), one of butter beans, and one of coffee. With rice, a salad, and a stack of Wonder bread, that made a fine breakfast after a long night of dancing and drinking.

Place the beans in a medium saucepan, cover with cold water by 2 inches, and place over high heat. Boil for 2 minutes, then remove from the heat and let soak for 1 hour.

Slice the sausage on a sharp diagonal into ½-inch lengths. Core the peppers and cut them into 1-inch pieces. Dice the celery and roughly chop the onion and garlic. Add the sausage, all the vegetables, and the bay leaf to a 6- to 7-quart slow cooker. Drain the beans and add them to the cooker. Pour in enough water to just cover the ingredients, about 1½ quarts. Cook, covered, on the low setting for about 6 hours, until the beans are soft and starting to break apart. With a large spoon, ladle off and discard some of the liquid if the mixture is too runny; stir the beans, smashing some of them against the side of the cooker insert to thicken the liquid. (Alternatively, scoot the sausage over to one side of the cooker and use an immersion or stick blender to break up some of the beans, or combine the flour with a bit of the liquid in a small cup and stir it into the beans.)

Season to taste with the cayenne, plenty of salt, and black pepper. Continue to cook, uncovered, on the high setting for 1 more hour.

Meanwhile, rinse the rice in several changes of cold water, until the water runs clear. Place in a 2-quart saucepan with 2 cups cold water and 1 teaspoon salt. Bring to a boil over medium heat, then cover the pot and lower the heat to the lowest possible temperature. Simmer for 14 minutes. Remove from the heat and fluff the rice with a fork. Re-cover the pot and let the rice sit for 5 minutes.

Spoon the rice onto individual serving plates and top with the beans and sausage. Serve hot.

RIBOLLITA (ITALIAN BREAD SOUP)

Serves 4 to 6
4-quart slow cooker

½ large onion

1 large carrot

2 ribs celery

2 cloves garlic

½ pound dried navy beans
(1¼ cups)

2 quarts vegetable stock
or water

1 bay leaf

1 sprig dried or fresh rosemary

1 large head escarole or other
bitter greens

2 thick slices crusty white bread
such as panella, cut into 1-inch
cubes (about 4 cups)

2 ripe tomatoes, chopped

½ bunch flat-leaf parsley,
stemmed and chopped

Salt and freshly ground
black pepper

3 tablespoons good-quality
extra-virgin olive oil

*When I worked at a publishing company on Park Avenue South in Manhattan,
I used to splurge (if several lunches a week can be called splurging) on big takeout
cups of ribollita from a nearby Italian restaurant, now defunct. This is a hearty
but colorful and fresh-tasting rendition, perfect for a winter lunch.*

Coarsely chop the onion, carrot, celery, and garlic and place the vegetables in a
4-quart slow cooker. Add the beans, stock, bay leaf, and rosemary and cook, covered,
on the low setting for 5 hours, until the beans are tender but still hold their shape.

Thoroughly wash the escarole and chop the leaves crosswise into 1-inch-wide strips;
add the escarole to the cooker, along with the bread, tomatoes, and parsley, and
stir gently to push the greens down into the liquid. Cover the cooker and continue
to cook on the high setting for 30 minutes, or until the greens are tender. Season
to taste with salt and plenty of pepper. Remove and discard the rosemary stem
and bay leaf and serve the soup in deep bowls, drizzled with the oil.

MAIN DISHES WITH MEAT, POULTRY & SEAFOOD

RENDANG PADANG (INDONESIAN BEEF CURRY)

Serves 6 to 8
4-quart slow cooker

3   pounds beef stew meat, cut into 1- to 2-inch chunks

8   fresh hot cayenne or other red chiles, stemmed and coarsely chopped

½   small onion, chopped

2   inches fresh ginger, peeled and chopped

3   cloves garlic, chopped

1   stalk lemongrass, tough outer layers removed, tender insides finely sliced

⅓   cup tamarind paste, mixed with ⅓ cup warm water

1   teaspoon ground cumin

1   teaspoon ground coriander

1   teaspoon ground turmeric

½   teaspoon chile powder

1   (15-ounce) can unsweetened coconut milk

2   teaspoons sugar

    Salt

    Steamed long-grain rice to serve

Serve this with steamed white rice, and Achar, the traditional accompaniment of vegetables (page 31).

Put the beef in a 4-quart slow cooker.

In a food processor or blender, combine the chiles, onion, ginger, garlic, lemongrass, tamarind paste, 1 cup warm water, and the spices. Process to a smooth puree, then pour it over the beef. Stir in the coconut milk. Cook, covered, on the low setting for 5 to 6 hours, until the beef is very tender and the sauce is a dark brown color.

Ladle most of the sauce into a small saucepan and cook over medium-high heat until slightly thickened and reduced, about 30 minutes, then pour it back into the cooker. Cook, uncovered, on the high setting for 30 minutes to 1 hour longer.

Stir in the sugar, then season with salt to taste. Serve with rice.

Pictured on page 80

CHOUCROUTE GARNIE

Serves 4
6- to 7-quart slow cooker

1 tablespoon vegetable oil
1 pound fresh Polish sausage, in links (see Note)
1 pound smoked kielbasa, cut into 3 or 4 lengths
2½ pounds pork chops
   Salt and freshly ground black pepper
1 cup dry white wine, or ½ cup dry vermouth plus ½ cup water
1 teaspoon juniper berries
1 pound sauerkraut, drained
1 tart apple, peeled, cored, and diced

Choucroute *means "sauerkraut" in French, but it's the "garnish" that really steals the show in this dish—especially if you make your own garlicky pork sausage.*

In a large skillet over medium-high heat, heat the oil and add the fresh and smoked sausages. Cook, turning, until the fresh sausage is browned on all sides, about 8 minutes. Transfer to a 6- to 7-quart slow cooker.

Season the pork chops on both sides with salt and pepper, then add them to the skillet and brown on both sides over medium-high heat for about 8 minutes. Transfer the chops to the cooker.

Return the skillet to high heat and pour in the wine and juniper berries, scraping up the browned bits from the bottom of the skillet. Bring to a boil and cook for 1 minute. Pour the liquid over the meats in the cooker. Cook, covered, on the low setting for about 3 hours, until the fresh sausage is cooked through.

Use tongs to remove the meats to a platter. Stir the sauerkraut and apple into the juices in the cooker. Arrange the meats on top of the sauerkraut, and cook until just heated through. Cover and cook on the high setting for about 30 minutes, until the apple is just soft and the sauerkraut is heated through. Season the sauerkraut to taste with salt and pepper, serve hot.

Note: I like to make my own pork sausage, and use some for this dish and freeze the rest. Coarsely grind 5 pounds not-too-lean pork shoulder meat and mix in 2 tablespoons salt, ½ tablespoon freshly ground black pepper, 1 teaspoon dried oregano, 5 cloves minced garlic, and ½ cup cold water. Stuff into hog casings (see Note, page 75) and twist at 4-inch intervals to form links.

BRACIOLE

Serves 4
4-quart slow cooker

2   tablespoons olive oil
2   eggs
4   large, thin slices beef top
    round (about 1½ pounds total)
3   ounces Parmesan cheese,
    grated (about ½ cup), plus
    more for serving
1   cup fresh flat-leaf parsley
    (stems removed), chopped
    Salt and freshly ground
    black pepper
4   cloves garlic, chopped
1   (28-ounce) can crushed
    tomatoes
2   large sprigs fresh basil
1   pound dried long pasta, such
    as spaghetti or linguine

Braciole are thinly sliced and pounded meat rolled up with a filling of some sort (it could be fresh herbs, a thin omelet, cooked spinach or other greens, sometimes even plumped raisins) and then simmered until the meat is cooked through and tender and the sauce is thick and flavorful. You can serve braciole by themselves or over pasta to soak up the sauce and meat juices.

Heat 1 teaspoon of the oil in a large nonstick sauté pan over high heat. Beat the eggs together with 2 teaspoons water, then pour them into the pan and swirl it to coat the bottom. Cook just until the omelet is set on both sides, about 4 minutes total. Use a spatula to cut the omelet into eighths, then remove from the pan and set aside.

Place one of the beef slices between two sheets of plastic wrap and pound with the flat side of a meat tenderizer until it's about ⅛ inch thick. Remove the top piece of plastic. Sprinkle with about 1 tablespoon of the cheese, top with 1 tablespoon parsley, then 2 pieces of the omelet, then 1 more tablespoon cheese. Sprinkle lightly with pepper. Starting at a narrow end, roll up the beef and secure it closed with toothpicks. Repeat with the remaining beef slices.

Heat the remaining oil in the sauté pan over medium-high heat, then add the beef rolls. Cook for about 8 minutes, turning with tongs, until lightly browned on all sides. Transfer the beef rolls to a 4-quart slow cooker, then add the garlic to the sauté pan and cook until just softened and beginning to brown, about 2 minutes. Pour in the tomatoes and half a can of water, bring to a boil, then pour the sauce into the cooker over the beef rolls. Stir in half of the basil and half of the remaining parsley, along with 1 teaspoon salt and ½ teaspoon pepper, then cook, covered, on the low setting for 5 hours, or until the beef rolls are tender, then remove the lid and cook on the high setting, uncovered, for 30 minutes, or until the sauce is thick. Season with salt and pepper to taste and stir in the remaining basil and parsley.

When ready to serve, cook the pasta in a large pot of boiling salted water until al dente. Drain and serve, topped with the braciole and sauce (remove the toothpicks, or warn your guests about them). Pass extra grated cheese at the table.

OSSO BUCO

Serves 4
6- to 7-quart slow cooker

4   slices veal shank, about 2½
    inches thick (1 large shank)
    Salt and freshly ground
    black pepper
    Flour for dredging
1   tablespoon olive oil
1   cup dry white wine
½   onion, diced
2   small carrots, diced
2   ribs celery, with leaves, diced
2   cloves garlic, chopped
4   sprigs fresh thyme, stems
    removed
½   (28-ounce) can plum tomatoes
½   cup pitted black olives
4   drained preserved artichoke
    hearts, cut into quarters
½   cup fresh flat-leaf parsley
    leaves
    Zest of 1 lemon, removed
    with a zester
    Zest of 1 orange, removed
    with a zester

Shank meat (you could also use lamb instead of veal) becomes velvety and tender when simmered slowly in a colorful fresh vegetable sauce. The classic osso buco topping, gremolata, usually consists of about equal parts parsley, lemon zest, and garlic, all minced together on a board; I prefer to omit the garlic and use orange zest in addition to the lemon. Serve the osso buco with a mound of polenta (page 48).

Tie each veal slice around its girth with kitchen string to hold it in a compact circle. Season the slices with salt and pepper, then dredge them in the flour, shaking off the excess. In a large skillet or sauté pan, heat the oil over medium-high heat. Add the veal slices, in one layer, and cook for 5 minutes on each side to brown well. Arrange the slices in a 6- to 7-quart slow cooker and return the skillet to high heat. Add the wine to the skillet and use a spatula to scrape up the browned bits on the bottom. Boil the wine for 2 minutes, then pour it over the veal.

Scatter the onion, carrots, celery, garlic, and thyme over the veal. Chop the tomatoes and add them, with their juices, to the cooker. Sprinkle 1 teaspoon salt and ½ teaspoon pepper over the vegetables and veal. Cook, covered, on the low setting for 4 to 5 hours, until the veal is tender and the vegetables are soft. Thirty minutes before the end of the cooking time, add the olives and artichoke hearts. Season to taste with salt and pepper.

To make the gremolata, very finely mince the parsley and zests together on a board. Remove the strings from the veal slices. Place one veal slice on each of 4 individual serving plates and spoon some of the sauce and vegetables over it. Sprinkle the gremolata on top and serve immediately.

LAMB TAGINE WITH GOLDEN RAISINS

Serves 4

4-quart slow cooker

3   pounds lamb stew meat (from the shoulder or leg)

1   clove garlic, smashed and peeled

2   tomatoes, chopped

1   tablespoon good-quality ground cinnamon

2   teaspoons sugar
    Salt and freshly ground black pepper

1   tablespoon tomato paste (optional; see Note)

1   bunch fresh cilantro

2   tablespoons butter

2   sweet onions, halved and thinly sliced

1½ teaspoons ground cumin

¾   cup golden raisins

2   cups instant couscous, cooked in lightly salted water and fluffed with a fork

This is a French Moroccan–inspired stew in which nuggets of lamb, redolent of cinnamon, are cooked until the meat is so tender it practically melts in your mouth. The raisins, and the caramelized onion topping, add a touch of sweetness, which is cut by the subtle acidity of tomato and the bright taste of fresh cilantro, stirred in at the last minute. This is best served with plain fluffy couscous.

If you have a small (1- or 2-quart) slow cooker in addition to a larger one, you can cook the onion topping in the small cooker instead of in a skillet: When you start to cook the lamb mixture in the larger cooker, place the butter and onion slices in the small one, sprinkle with the cumin, salt, and pepper, and cook on the low setting for 5 to 6 hours.

Place the lamb in a 4-quart slow cooker and add the garlic, tomatoes, cinnamon, sugar, 1 teaspoon salt, ½ teaspoon pepper, ½ cup water, and the tomato paste, if using. Keeping the cilantro in a bunch, cut off the stems and tie them together with kitchen string; set the leaves aside. Nestle the bundle of stems into the ingredients in the slow cooker. Cook on the low setting for 5 to 6 hours, or until the lamb is very tender, then remove and discard the cilantro stems.

Meanwhile, put the butter, onions, and cumin in a medium skillet or sauté pan and cook over low heat, stirring occasionally, until the onion is very soft and deep golden brown, about 30 minutes. Season with salt and pepper to taste, then remove from the heat.

Twenty minutes before the end of the cooking time for the lamb, remove the lid and skim off as much of the clear fat from the surface of the stew as possible. Reserving a few sprigs for garnish, roughly chop the cilantro leaves and stir them, along with the raisins, into the lamb; continue to cook, uncovered on the high setting, for 20 minutes. Taste and season with salt and pepper as necessary. Spoon the couscous onto a serving platter or individual plates and top with the lamb and the caramelized onion and reserved cilantro sprigs.

Note: If the fresh tomato isn't top quality, ripe and red, use a little tomato paste to enhance the flavor of the tagine: Stir it into the water when you load up the slow cooker.

CARNE ADOBADA WITH RED CHILE

Serves 4

4   ounces dried red chiles
    (see Note)
2   cloves garlic
½   onion, roughly chopped
½   teaspoon dried oregano
1   tablespoon honey
    Salt and freshly ground black
    pepper
    One (6-pound) pork shoulder
1   tablespoon vegetable oil

My guy and I recently drove from Reno to Albuquerque, and needless to say we sampled as much food as we possibly could along the way—from grilled Basque lamb in Elko, Nevada, to "scones" with "Honey and Butter Flavored Topping" in Salina, Utah (among the many things to find annoying about Utah is its twisted nomenclature), to carne adobada (marinated pork) in about half a dozen restaurants in and around Derek's old stomping grounds of Albuquerque. We both especially liked the smoky red chile of the carne adobada we had for breakfast one rainy morning at the lovely Barela's Coffee Shop downtown, which had distinct bits of charred chiles in it, and we appreciated the larger chunks of pork in the version of the same dish we had at Sadie's, a sprawling, bustling mega restaurant in the northeast quarter. This recipe combines the best aspects of each.

Should authenticity be your aim, serve the pork and chile with coarsely grated cheddar cheese melting over the top (everything in New Mexico has cheddar cheese on top of it—which made me think we should just move there already), and toasty flour tortillas on the side. Of course, if your table also were to feature a basket of freshly fried sopaipillas, and if refried beans, rice, corn tortillas, and a couple of fried eggs, over medium, were to find their way onto your plate, you'd be getting warmer.

If you'd like, double the quantities for the chile puree (8 ounces chiles, 4 cloves garlic, 1 onion, 1 teaspoon oregano, 1 tablespoon salt, 4 cups water)—this amount will just fit in the average blender. Put half of the sauce in a pan and simmer over low heat for about 1 hour, puree again (let the sauce cool before turning on the blender—I'm still cleaning up the mess I made the first time I tried to puree steaming hot chile), then season with salt if necessary. Let the chile cool to room temperature and freeze it for later; spoon hot chile over huevos rancheros or use it in enchiladas.

Break the chiles into pieces and shake out most of the seeds; discard the stems and seeds and rinse the chiles in warm water. Heat a heavy skillet over medium-high heat and, working in batches, add the chiles. Toast, turning the chiles frequently, for about 5 minutes, until blackened in spots. Transfer the chiles to a blender. Add the garlic and onion to the skillet and cook, turning frequently, for about 5 minutes, until blackened in spots. Add to the blender, along with 2 cups water, the oregano, honey, and 2 teaspoons salt. Blend to a very smooth puree. Set aside.

Trim the excess fat from the pork (including the thick layer of fat and skin on the underside). If it looks like the shoulder won't fit in your slow cooker whole, cut off a hunk or two so that you'll be able to nestle the pieces snugly in the cooker insert. Score the meat about ½ inch deep in several places with a sharp knife and season the meat all over with salt and pepper. Heat the oil in the skillet over medium-high heat and add the pork. Cook until nicely browned on all sides, about 10 minutes total. Using tongs, transfer the pork to a 4-quart slow cooker. Return the skillet to the heat and pour in ½ cup water, scraping up the browned bits with a spatula. Pour the water over the pork in the cooker, then pour in the chile puree.

Cook, covered, on the low setting for 6 to 8 hours, until the pork is very tender. During the last hour of the cooking time, remove the lid and turn the cooker to high. Using tongs, remove the pork to a cutting board. Cut the meat into large chunks and discard the bones. Skim off some of the fat that's risen to the surface of the sauce. If it's still too liquidy—it should be a good bit runnier than the original uncooked chile puree—use an immersion (stick) blender to further puree and thicken the chile; blending also serves to emulsify the fat in the sauce so that it's velvety smooth. (If using a regular blender, ladle some of the sauce into the blender, let it cool, then blend, starting on the lowest possible speed, until smooth and thick; scrape the sauce back into the cooker.) Season to taste with salt if necessary. Return the meat to the sauce and cook, covered, until heated through. Serve the meat hot, with plenty of the chile sauce.

Note: In the absence of true New Mexico chiles, I use a combination of wrinkly, dark, almost black mulatos, smooth, deep red guajillos, and a few small arbol chiles for extra heat. If your chile puree tastes unbearably hot before it's been cooked, don't worry: A day in the slow cooker will take care of that. You might even need to add some pure chile powder at the end to spice it up a bit.

CHICKEN & DUMPLINGS

Serves 4 to 6
4-quart slow cooker

For the chicken:

½ cup flour

Salt and freshly ground black pepper

3 pounds bone-in chicken thighs and legs, skin and most of the fat removed

2 tablespoons olive oil

6 medium leeks, white and light green parts only

1 fennel bulb, trimmed, upper stalks removed, fronds reserved for garnish

1½ teaspoons fresh thyme leaves

2 tablespoons minced fresh flat-leaf parsley

Parsley sprigs for garnish

For the dumplings:

2 cups all-purpose flour

4 teaspoons baking powder

½ teaspoon salt

2 tablespoons minced fresh flat-leaf parsley

1 cup milk

½ teaspoon freshly ground black pepper

¼ teaspoon salt

This is a somewhat unusual, but still very comforting, version of the classic celery-carrot-pea dish. Here I leave the bones in the chicken pieces for more flavor, but you could use boneless thighs and substitute chicken stock for the water.

Prepare the chicken: In a shallow dish, combine the flour with 1 teaspoon salt and ½ teaspoon pepper. Dredge the chicken pieces in the seasoned flour. In a large skillet or sauté pan, heat 1 tablespoon of the oil over medium-high heat, then add the chicken pieces. Cook until thoroughly browned, about 5 minutes on each side; transfer to a 4-quart slow cooker.

Meanwhile, slice the leeks into ½-inch rounds and wash and drain them well. Cut the fennel in half vertically, cut out the tough core, then cut the fennel crosswise into ½-inch slices. Return the skillet to medium-high heat and add the remaining 1 tablespoon oil. Add the leeks, fennel, and 2 tablespoons of the dredging flour. Cook, stirring frequently and scraping up the browned bits from cooking the chicken, for about 5 minutes, until the vegetables are slightly softened and the flour is cooked and golden brown. Add 1½ cups of water and bring to a boil, stirring. Pour the vegetables and liquid into the cooker over the chicken. Cook, covered, on the low setting for 3½ to 4 hours, until the vegetables are soft and the chicken is falling off the bone and tender. If the liquid is too runny, spoon a ¼ cup of it into a measuring cup and whisk in 1 tablespoon flour, then pour it back into the cooker. Stir in the thyme and minced parsley and add more salt and pepper to taste, as necessary.

Prepare the dumplings: In a medium bowl, combine the flour, baking powder, salt, and parsley with a fork, then add the milk. Stir with the fork until the dry ingredients are just combined and moistened—do not overmix the dough. Use a large spoon to gently scoop ½-cup dollops of dumpling dough onto the surface of the gravy in the cooker. Sprinkle the tops of the dumplings with the pepper and salt. Cook, uncovered, on the high setting, for 5 minutes, then replace the lid and cook for 25 to 30 minutes longer, until the dumplings are cooked through and fluffy; a toothpick inserted in the center of a dumpling will come out clean. Serve in large bowls, garnished with the parsley sprigs and reserved fennel fronds.

CURRIED CHICKEN ROTI

Serves 4
4-quart slow cooker

2   pounds chicken thighs
1   tablespoon vegetable oil
2   teaspoons curry powder
½   teaspoon chile powder
     Salt and freshly ground
     black pepper
3   russet potatoes, peeled and
     cut into ¾-inch chunks
1   small onion, chopped
2   cloves garlic, chopped
½   pound green beans, topped
     and tailed and cut into 1-inch
     lengths
     Habanero hot sauce or
     chopped fresh hot chiles
     (optional)
     Roti (recipe follows)

My mom and dad lived for several months in Suriname, a former Dutch colony on the northern coast of South America. While my dad worked to help the government clean up mining operations in the nearly uninhabited interior, my mom had very little to do besides hand-hem countless batik tablecloths and napkins—and go to a local roti hut to learn how to make the flatbreads from the cooks there. It took her a while, but she was finally able to replicate those roti at home back in Virginia. The roti recipe that follows is hers.

Remove the skin and excess fat from the chicken thighs and cut out the bones, dropping the bones into a small pot of about 3 cups simmering water as you work and cutting the meat of each thigh into about three pieces.

In a large sauté pan, heat the oil over high heat and add the chicken, curry powder, and chile powder; sprinkle with salt and pepper. Cook, stirring, until the chicken is no longer pink on the outside, but not yet browned, about 4 minutes. Transfer the chicken to a 4-quart slow cooker. Add the potatoes, onion, and garlic in a layer over the chicken. Skim the foam off the top of the simmering chicken stock and pour 2 cups of the stock through a fine-mesh sieve into the cooker, so that it almost covers the ingredients. Cook, covered, on the low setting for 4 to 6 hours, until the potatoes are falling apart and thickening the liquids.

Bring a small saucepan of salted water to a boil and drop in the green beans. Boil for 4 to 5 minutes, until bright green and crisp-tender; drain and gently stir the beans into the curry mixture. Taste and season with more salt and pepper as necessary. Serve big spoonfuls of the curried chicken and potatoes, with hot sauce or chiles if desired, wrapped in the roti.

Makes 8

3 to 3½ cups self-rising flour
    (see Notes)
1   cup all-purpose flour
8   teaspoons besan (see Notes)
2   tablespoons vegetable oil

Roti

In a large bowl, combine 2 cups of the self-rising flour with 1¼ cups water and stir to make a sticky, wet mass. Add 1 to 1½ cups more self-rising flour and mix until the dough comes together. Turn the dough out onto a work surface dusted with some of the all-purpose flour and knead until the ball of dough is smooth but still very soft. Divide into 8 balls. Flatten each ball slightly and put 1 teaspoon of the besan in the center of each, then fold the edges up over the besan and pinch them together to enclose the besan completely. Roll each ball in the oil and set aside to rest, covered with a clean towel, for 10 minutes.

Using a rolling pin, on a work surface generously dusted with all-purpose flour, roll out one of the balls into a thin round about 10 inches in diameter, taking care not to rupture the besan enclosure. Heat a large, heavy skillet or sauté pan over high heat, then carefully transfer the dough round to the pan. Cook, covered, for 1 to 2 minutes on each side, until puffed and speckled with dark brown spots. Put the roti in a towel-lined sealable container and immediately cover the container (or just wrap the roti in a towel). Continue with the remaining dough balls. Serve immediately, or reheat the roti for a few minutes in a steamer over simmering water.

Notes: If you don't have self-rising flour, for each 1 cup self-rising flour, use 1 cup all-purpose flour plus 1½ teaspoons baking powder and ⅛ teaspoon salt.

Besan is finely ground yellow chickpeas and is available in Southeast Asian markets. You can substitute fine yellow cornmeal if you grind it still more finely in a spice mill (it should have the texture of fish fry).

FESENJEN (CHICKEN WITH WALNUTS & POMEGRANATE)

Serves 4

4-quart slow cooker

2   pounds chicken thighs
    (about 8), skin and excess
    fat removed

3   cups walnuts

1   bay leaf

½   cup sugar

⅓   cup pomegranate molasses
    (see Note)

½   cup fresh pomegranate seeds
    or dried barberries

Serve this rich sweet-sour braised chicken dish over plain basmati rice or, better, Persian rice with a shard of tahdig *(the buttery crust that forms on the bottom of the skillet as Persian rice cooks).*

You'll notice that there's no salt in this dish: It simply isn't necessary. Sometimes I use low-sodium chicken stock instead of the water and bay leaf, but the flavor is just as deep and complex with plain water.

Put the chicken thighs in a 4-quart slow cooker.

In a large skillet, toast the walnuts over medium-high heat, stirring constantly, for 3 minutes. Transfer the walnuts to a food processor and finely chop them. Add the walnuts and bay leaf to the cooker. Pour in 1⅔ cups water and cook, covered, on the low setting for 3 to 4 hours, until the chicken is tender.

Using tongs, remove the chicken thighs to a board and pull the meat off the bones in large chunks; set the meat aside.

Turn the cooker to the high setting. Stir the sugar and pomegranate molasses into the sauce and cook, uncovered, for 1 hour, until the sauce is thickened and simmering. (If you prefer a much thicker sauce, pour it into a large saucepan and bring to a full boil over high heat; boil for 20 to 25 minutes, then add the chicken to the sauce and cook to heat through.) Return the chicken to the sauce and cook until heated through; retrieve and discard the bay leaf. Serve hot, sprinkled with the pomegranate seeds.

Note: Pomegranate molasses (or concentrate) is available in bottles in Middle Eastern food stores. The best ones are those made in Lebanon.

CHICKEN IN MOLE VERDE

Serves 4
4-quart slow cooker

1   pound tomatillos
4   fresh green jalapeño or
    serrano chiles
½   white onion
4   cloves garlic
1   cup pepitas (hulled pumpkin
    seeds)
    Salt and freshly ground black
    pepper
1   pound chicken thighs and legs
1   cup packed fresh cilantro leaves
    Leaves of 1 bunch radishes
    (about 2 cups leaves), tough
    stems removed

Serve this tangy, spicy chicken and its sauce with a big mound of plain white rice, warmed corn tortillas, and, if you like, a bowl of thinly sliced radishes and lemon or lime wedges on the side.

Preheat the broiler and line a rimmed sheet pan with aluminum foil.

Remove the papery husks from the tomatillos and rinse the tomatillos; place them on the prepared sheet pan. Cut the stems off the chiles and add them, along with the onion and garlic, to the sheet pan. Broil, about 4 inches from the heat source, for 4 to 5 minutes, until the tomatillos are well browned on top; use tongs to turn the vegetables over and broil for another 4 to 5 minutes. Set aside to cool slightly.

In a medium sauté pan over medium-high heat, toast the pepitas until a few of them are just beginning to brown and most of them have popped and expanded. Transfer to a blender and add the broiled vegetables and any juices from the sheet pan, 2 teaspoons salt, and 1 teaspoon pepper. Blend to a smooth puree.

Pull the skin off the chicken pieces and discard it; trim off as much excess fat as you can and place the chicken in a 4-quart slow cooker. Pour in the tomatillo puree and turn the chicken to coat the pieces. Cook, covered, on the low setting for 4 to 5 hours, until the chicken is cooked through and tender but not yet falling off the bones.

Spoon about 1½ cups of the sauce back into the blender and add the cilantro and radish leaves. Blend to a smooth puree and scrape the sauce back into the cooker, stirring to incorporate the herbs. Cook, with the lid askew, on the high setting for about 1 hour longer, until the sauce has thickened and the chicken is very tender. Season with salt and pepper to taste, then serve hot.

DORO WAT (ETHIOPIAN BRAISED CHICKEN)

Serves 2 to 4
4-quart slow cooker

½   white onion, roughly diced

4   cloves garlic

1   1-inch piece fresh ginger, peeled and chopped

½   cup Berber spice mix (see Note)
     Salt

2   tablespoons vegetable oil

1   pound chicken legs and thighs

½   cup dry red wine

3   tablespoons butter or Ghee (page 50)

2   hard-cooked eggs, peeled
     Injera (recipe follows)

A little doro wat goes a long way—it's extremely spicy, flavorful, and buttery. Serve a couple of pieces of the chicken, half an egg, and the sauce on top of a large injera, *with a small mound of tender, slowly braised kale or cabbage, and perhaps some Berber-spiced stewed lentils alongside the chicken for a full Ethiopian-style meal.*

Put the onion, garlic, ginger, spice mix, 1 teaspoon salt, 1 tablespoon of the oil, and 2 tablespoons water in a mini food processor and puree, adding more water if necessary, to attain a barely pourable paste.

Pull off the skin and trim any excess fat from the chicken pieces and season them lightly with salt. Heat the remaining oil in a large sauté pan over high heat. Add the chicken pieces and cook until light golden, about 4 minutes on each side. Transfer the pieces to a 4-quart slow cooker. Return the pan to high heat and pour in the wine; boil for 1 minute, then stir in the spice paste and immediately remove from the heat. Pour the wine mixture into the cooker and turn the chicken pieces to coat them with the sauce. Add the butter. Cook, covered, on the low setting for 4 hours, or until the chicken is tender but not yet falling off the bone. Stir gently to incorporate the thicker sauce at the bottom of the cooker and season with salt to taste if necessary.

With a paring knife, score the eggs lightly all over, then nestle them in the sauce; cook, covered, until heated through, about 20 more minutes. Serve hot, in shallow bowls, with the *injera* underneath or on the side. Tear off pieces of the *injera* to use instead of a fork to scoop up bits of the chicken meat, egg, and sauce.

Note: To make Berber spice mix, put 12 stemmed and seeded hot dried red chiles (such as arbol or cayenne), 2 teaspoons fenugreek seeds, 2 teaspoons whole black peppercorns, 1 teaspoon cumin seeds, 1 teaspoon ajowan seeds (optional), ½ teaspoon allspice berries, ½ teaspoon whole cloves, and 8 crushed white cardamom pods in a small sauté pan. Toast over medium-high heat, stirring frequently, until fragrant but not browned, about 3 minutes. Transfer to a spice mill or coffee grinder and grind to a fine powder. Stir in 2 teaspoons paprika and 1 teaspoon ground ginger. This makes about ½ cup.

INJERA (ETHIOPIAN SOURDOUGH FLATBREAD)

Serves 4

1 teaspoon honey

1 scant tablespoon active dry yeast

2 cups self-rising flour

¾ cup whole-wheat flour

2 teaspoons salt

1 tablespoon baking powder

Injera *is traditionally made with deep-brown, very-low-gluten teff, the smallest grain in the world. Teff and teff flour are a bit hard to find in this country (see Sources), but whole-wheat flour works well too, and yields* injera *that tastes very much like that served at Ethiopian restaurants. (I suspect that most restaurants here use whole-wheat flour.) Be sure to start the* injera *batter at least a day in advance so it has time to become sour.*

In a large bowl, combine 2½ cups warm water and the honey and sprinkle the yeast over the water; stir well. Add the flours and stir to form a wet batter. Cover the bowl loosely with plastic wrap and let stand at room temperature for at least 24 hours or up to 3 days. (The longer it stands, the more sour the *injera* will be.)

Scrape the dough into a blender and add ½ cup warm water, the salt, and the baking powder. Blend just until the mixture is smooth and runny, like a very thin pancake batter. Add more water if necessary.

Heat a large nonstick sauté pan over medium-high heat. Pour about ½ cup of the batter into the pan and quickly swirl the pan to thinly coat the bottom with batter. Cook for about 2 minutes, or until bubbles appear on the surface in the center of the pancake and the top appears dry all over; do not let the bottom brown. Use a thin spatula to transfer each flatbread to a plate lined with a clean towel, and wrap with the towel while you make the remaining *injera*.

TUNA POACHED IN EXTRA-VIRGIN OLIVE OIL

Serves 4
4-quart slow cooker

For the tuna:

About 3 cups extra-virgin olive oil

2   bay leaves

¼   teaspoon whole black peppercorns

4   (1-inch-thick) pieces tuna steak (about 2¼ pounds)

2   small carrots, finely diced

2   ribs celery, finely diced

½   cup drained caperberries with stems, preserved in vinegar

For the sauce:

1   large egg yolk

2   tablespoons vinegar reserved from the caperberries

1   teaspoon grainy mustard

⅓   cup extra-virgin olive oil reserved from cooking the tuna

Salt and freshly ground black pepper

Slowly poaching tuna in oil until relatively well done is, according to cookbook author Mark Bittman, a common method of cooking the meaty fish in Italy. It's difficult to maintain such a low heat level on the stovetop, but in a slow cooker, low is as high as it gets. The sauce uses raw egg yolk; if you aren't confident that the eggs from your market are very fresh, simply omit the egg yolk and use a touch more oil to thicken the sauce.

Make the tuna: Put the oil, bay leaves, and peppercorns in a 4-quart slow cooker and cook, covered, on the high setting for 45 minutes.

Lower the tuna into the oil, arranging the pieces in one layer so that they're just covered by the oil; add a bit more oil if necessary. Cook, covered, on the high setting for 30 to 45 minutes, until the tuna is evenly colored but still pink on the inside.

Meanwhile, heat 1 teaspoon of the oil in a small sauté pan over medium heat and add the carrots, celery, and caperberries. Sauté until the vegetables are tender-crisp and starting to brown, 8 to 10 minutes. Set aside.

Make the sauce: While the tuna is cooking, combine the egg yolk, vinegar, and mustard in a mini food processor or blender. With the motor running, slowly add the oil in a thin stream. The sauce will become creamy and will thicken slightly. Season to taste with salt and pepper.

Use tongs to transfer the tuna steaks to a board lined with paper towels and pat them dry. Move the tuna steaks to 4 individual serving plates and spoon the sautéed vegetables over them. Spoon the sauce over all and serve immediately.

SALMON WITH BABY ZUCCHINI & BASIL

Serves 4
6- to 7-quart slow cooker

4   (6-ounce) pieces salmon fillet,
    with skin, about ¾ inch thick
    in the center
    Salt and freshly ground
    black pepper
1   tender top sprigs fresh basil,
    stems removed
8   baby zucchini
4   teaspoons extra-virgin olive oil
4   thin rounds lemon
    Coarse sea salt

These pretty little fillets aren't slow-cooked at all, but take advantage of the cooker's low and even temperature, which is perfect for foods that need gentle cooking. Serve the fresh fillets with a mound of Herbed Mashed Potatoes (page 36), Wild Rice with Cherries and Orange (page 42), or plain buttered white rice.

Put a wire rack and 1 cup water in a 6- to 7-quart slow cooker and preheat, covered, while you prepare the salmon packets.

Place a piece of aluminum foil on a work surface and lay one piece of salmon fillet in the center, skin side down. Season lightly with salt and pepper. Lay the basil leaves on top of the fillet. Slice the zucchini very thinly lengthwise and arrange the slices evenly over the basil to completely cover the top of the fillet. Drizzle with 1 teaspoon of the oil and season lightly with salt and pepper. Place a lemon slice on top. Fold up the edges of the foil and crimp them together to seal the packet tightly. Repeat with the remaining salmon, basil, zucchini, oil, and lemon.

Set the packets on the rack in the cooker and quickly replace the lid. Cook on the high setting for 20 minutes. Use tongs to remove the packets to a work surface and gently open them. Slide a thin metal spatula underneath the salmon fillet, between the flesh and the skin, and lift the fillet off the skin and onto a serving plate. Repeat with the remaining packets, season each fillet with a pinch of sea salt, and serve immediately.

CIOPPINO

2 tablespoons extra-virgin olive oil

1 carrot, diced

2 ribs celery, diced

½ onion, diced

1 shallot, diced

3 cloves garlic, 2 minced, 1 cut in half

2 dried hot chiles, stems removed, crumbled

4 anchovy fillets, drained and minced

1 cup dry white wine

1½ cups fish stock (see Tip)

½ (28-ounce) can peeled plum tomatoes, drained, seeded, and diced

1 tablespoon tomato paste

1 bay leaf
    Freshly ground black pepper

¼ cup chopped fresh flat-leaf parsley

    About 5 pounds cleaned fish and shellfish (see Note)
    Salt

1 baguette

Cioppino is a specialty of Genoans in San Francisco, and it's a riotous stew of all kinds of seafood cooked with vegetables, wine, and tomatoes (much like a bouillabaisse). My Uncle Jim makes it every year as soon as Dungeness crab comes into season in mid-November (the season lasts through May on the West Coast) and is readily available.

In a medium sauté pan or skillet over medium-high heat, heat 1 tablespoon of the oil. Add the carrot, celery, onion, shallot, minced garlic, chiles, and anchovies and cook, stirring frequently, until the onion is beginning to soften but not brown, about 6 minutes. Pour in the wine and bring to a boil; cook until the wine is reduced by half, then scrape the vegetable mixture into a 4-quart slow cooker. Stir in the stock, tomatoes, and tomato paste, and add the bay leaf and ½ teaspoon black pepper. Cook, covered, on the low setting for 3 to 4 hours, until the carrot and celery are soft.

Stir in the parsley and season to taste with salt and pepper as necessary. Arrange the fish and shellfish over the tomato stew (put squid and octopus [if using] in first, then whole fish and fillets, then crab legs and shellfish), turn the cooker to the high setting, and cook, covered, without lifting the lid, for 30 minutes, or until the shellfish shells open (discard any clams or mussels that do not open after 30 minutes) and the fish flakes easily with a fork.

Meanwhile, preheat the oven to 350°F. Slice the baguette into 3-inch lengths and split each in half horizontally. Brush the cut sides with the remaining 1 tablespoon oil, sprinkle with salt and pepper, and rub with the cut sides of the halved garlic clove. Bake for 15 minutes, or until lightly browned and crisp.

Ladle the stew into shallow bowls and serve with the toasted baguette on the side.

Note: *Use any combination of small cleaned whole fish such as smelts and sardines; filletted larger white-fleshed fish such as porgies, roughy, sea bass, or red snapper; Dungeness, snow, or king crab legs (thawed if frozen, and chopped into 2-inch lengths with a cleaver); scrubbed mussels and clams; and cleaned and sliced small squid and octopus.*

Making Fish Stock

Ask your fishmonger to give you the fish heads and other trimmings after he or she cleans whole fish for you (or clean your own and save the trimmings). To make a quick fish stock, put the trimmings in a medium saucepan of water, along with 1 roughly chopped celery rib, 1 roughly chopped carrot, ½ onion, and a few peppercorns. Simmer, skimming the foam from the surface once or twice, for 30 minutes. Pour through a fine-mesh sieve into a measuring cup.

CAHUITA RON DON

About 1½ pounds salt cod fillets (from 2 dried fish, soaked for 12 to 24 hours in two changes of cold water)

1   small yucca (cassava)

1   green plantain

2   small green bell peppers

2   plum tomatoes

3   scallions

2   Scotch bonnet chiles (see page 24)

Handful of fresh thyme sprigs, tied together in a bundle, plus a few sprigs for garnish

4   cloves garlic, 2 crushed and 2 thinly sliced

2   (13.5-ounce) cans unsweetened coconut milk

1   small ripe yellow plantain
Freshly ground black pepper

1   tablespoon olive oil

My family and I once spent a few days in the small Costa Rican village of Cahuita, on the Jamaican-inflected Caribbean coast, in an open-air cabin a few steps from a black-sand beach, which was deserted in the rainy season. The one restaurant (and perhaps the one established business) in the village was called Miss Edith's, and if you wanted to eat there in the evening you had to tell her in the morning what you wanted. Most people, as far as we could tell, wanted her ron don. This is how I remember Miss Edith's version of the traditional dish.

I use soaked salt cod in this recipe, but you can use soaked salted mackerel, or even fresh firm white fish fillets such as cod or grouper; if you use fresh fish, add it with the yellow plantain toward the end of the cooking time.

Trim the skin and any very large bones from the fish and cut the fillets into 2- to 3-inch chunks; set aside in a bowl of cold water.

Peel the yucca, slice it into ¼-inch rounds, and add the yucca to a 4-quart slow cooker. Slice the plantain into ¼-inch rounds, peel the slices, and add the plantain to the cooker. Core the bell peppers, cut them into 2-inch pieces, and add them to the cooker. Dice the tomatoes and sprinkle them over the peppers. Slice the scallions and add the white and light green parts to the cooker (set the greens aside). Seed and mince the chiles and add them to the cooker. Tuck the thyme bundle and crushed garlic into the vegetables in the cooker, and lay the fish over the vegetables. Pour the coconut milk over all. Cook, covered, on the high setting for about 4 hours, until all the vegetables are soft but still hold their shape.

Peel and cut the yellow plantain on the diagonal into 1½-inch slices; add it to the cooker. Cook, covered, on the high setting for about 30 minutes, until the yellow plantain is very soft and the broth has thickened slightly. Season with pepper to taste (you shouldn't need to add any salt, as the cod retains a great deal of its saltiness even after a day's soaking).

In a small skillet, heat the oil over medium heat. Add the sliced garlic and sauté until just beginning to color, then drizzle the oil and garlic into the stew in the cooker. Remove and discard the thyme bundle, then ladle the ron don into wide serving bowls and garnish with scallion greens and fresh thyme sprigs. Serve immediately.

DESSERTS & OTHER SWEETS

VANILLA-COCONUT RICE PUDDING WITH SAUTÉED PAPAYA

Serves 6
4-quart slow cooker

1   cup basmati rice
1   (13.5-ounce) can unsweetened
    coconut milk (see Notes)
¾   cup plus 1 tablespoon sugar
    Pinch of salt
½   vanilla bean
1   cup half-and-half
1   large egg yolk
½   papaya, seeded, peeled, and
    sliced ¼ inch thick
4   teaspoons fried mung beans
    for garnish (optional;
    see Notes)

Until a few years ago, the only rice pudding I'd known was the super-thick, almost sliceable kind, with raisins and cinnamon, and I had no special fondness for the stuff. But then my good friend Jen made a soft, milky, chilled rice pudding topped with caramelized bananas for a New Year's Eve dinner, and I've never been the same. This slow-cooker rice pudding with coconut milk has that same soft, milky consistency. The crunchy-crisp fried mung beans are a nod to Wondee Siam, my favorite Thai restaurant here in New York, where they're sprinkled on sticky rice with mangoes.

In a 4-quart slow cooker, combine the rice, coconut milk, ¾ cup of the sugar, and the salt. Fill the coconut-milk can with water and add it to the cooker. Split the vanilla bean lengthwise and scrape the seeds into the cooker; drop the vanilla bean pods in too. Stir to combine. Cook, covered, on the low setting for 2 to 2½ hours, until the rice is soft and the mixture is thick; do not stir as it cooks. There will be a hollow filled with clear coconut oil in the center of the pudding; spoon the oil out and discard it, reserving 2 tablespoons for sautéing the papaya.

In a small bowl, combine ½ cup of the half-and-half and the egg yolk, then gradually pour it into the pudding, stirring constantly. Stir for 1 minute, then remove the vanilla bean pods (rinse them and pat them dry with a paper towel—they can be used again, or nestled in a bowl of granulated sugar to perfume it). Transfer the pudding to a large bowl, stir in the remaining ½ cup half-and-half, and let it cool to room temperature. Cover and chill in the refrigerator for at least 3 hours or up to 6 hours (after a day it starts to become runny).

Heat the reserved oil in a large skillet over medium-high heat. Add the papaya slices and remaining 1 tablespoon sugar and sauté, turning occasionally, for about 6 minutes, until soft and caramelized.

Scoop the chilled rice pudding onto dessert plates and top with the sautéed papaya. Sprinkle with the fried mung beans, if using.

Pictured on page 108

Notes: For this dish, use coconut milk that has a thick layer of solids at the top; otherwise the oil won't separate out during slow cooking. I use the Thai Chaokoh brand because it's good and also because it's inexpensive. If you find that no oil pools in the center of the rice as it cooks that's fine— just use butter to sauté the papaya.

Fried mung beans are available in the snacks section of Southeast Asian markets and grocers, with the rice puffs and so on. You can also just buy dried peeled split mung beans (available in Asian grocery stores) and fry them yourself: Heat a couple of inches of oil in a saucepan and put a tablespoon or so of the beans in a metal sieve and lower them into the hot oil; cook until golden brown and crisp, then drain on paper towels. Leftover fried mung beans (you'll have a lot if you buy a bag of prefried ones) are great in snack mixes with dried fruits, nuts, pepitas, and roasted chickpeas.

THAI DESSERT STEW

Serves 6 to 8
4-quart slow cooker

3   (13.5-ounce) cans unsweetened coconut milk

3   tablespoons palm (coconut) sugar

½   kabocha squash, scrubbed (not peeled), seeds and membranes removed

½   small yucca (cassava), peeled

1   sweet potato (such as a white Japanese or garnet sweet potato), peeled

4   small taro roots, stems removed, peeled

½   pound firm melon (such as casaba or orange-fleshed honeydew), peeled, seeds and membranes removed (optional)

Any combination of hard squashes and tubers you wish can be used instead of the ones listed here: Pumpkin is excellent, as is butternut and acorn squash, and regular sweet potatoes or yams.

Combine the coconut milk and palm sugar in a 4-quart slow cooker. Chop all the vegetables and the melon, if using, into ¾-inch chunks and add them to the cooker. Cook, covered, on the low setting for 3 to 4 hours, until all the vegetables are tender. Stir to disperse the solids and foam on the surface, then serve in small dessert bowls.

CHEWY-FUDGY BROWNIES

Serves 6 to 8

½ cup (1 stick) butter

2 ounces unsweetened chocolate, chopped

½ cup brown sugar

½ cup granulated sugar

2 large eggs
Pinch of salt

½ cup all-purpose flour

½ teaspoon vanilla extract

2 ounces bittersweet chocolate, chopped into large chunks

1 cup pecans, broken into large pieces (optional)

Vanilla ice cream, for serving (optional)

I honestly didn't think brownies could be made in a slow cooker, but these are quite excellent. The moist, low heat keeps the cake from drying out while letting it bake long enough to fully melt the chocolate chunks (try white chocolate, too, which leaves pockets of buttery liquor in the brownies). I like chewy brownies (as opposed to cakey, crumbly ones), and I like dense chocolate cakes: These brownies satisfy both desires, with their chewy edges and rich, fudgy centers.

Preheat a slow cooker, large enough to hold an 8-inch round or square baking pan, on the high setting. Grease the baking pan.

In a small saucepan over low heat, melt the unsweetened chocolate and butter together. Transfer the mixture to a medium bowl and stir in the sugars. Add the eggs, one at a time, beating well after each addition, then add the salt and flour and stir to combine. Stir in the vanilla, bittersweet chocolate, and pecans, if using. Pour the batter into the prepared pan and place on a rack in the cooker. Set two layers of paper towels over the top of the cooker and put the lid over the towels (this will keep moisture from dripping from the lid onto the cake). Bake on the high setting for 1 hour and 45 minutes to 2 hours, until a toothpick inserted in the center comes out clean—the center of the cake will still look wet and bubbly on top.

Carefully remove the pan from the cooker and let it cool on a wire rack for 15 minutes, then loosen the edge of the cake with a thin knife and turn it out onto a board. Serve wedges or squares—with ice cream, if desired.

DOUBLE-CHOCOLATE APRICOT BREAD PUDDING

Serves 6
4-quart slow cooker

1   round loaf crusty white bread
1   cup dried apricots, halved
    (see Notes)
½   cup brandy
3   tablespoons butter, softened
2   ounces bittersweet chocolate,
    roughly chopped
3   large eggs
1   cup whole milk
1   cup heavy cream
½   cup plus 1 teaspoon sugar
    Pinch of salt
½   teaspoon ground cinnamon
1   tablespoon cacao nibs
    (see Notes)
    Brandy Sauce (recipe follows)

This is also delicious with dried cherries or raisins instead of apricots. My fella, Derek, eats bites of the buttery top layer as it's cooking in the pot, and can't be bothered to wait for the egg to set up, much less for the brandy sauce to be added. The sauce might seem like overkill, but do try it if you want to make this classic country dessert a little bit city.

Preheat the oven to 250°F.

Cut the bread into 1-inch cubes and place them in one layer on a half-sheet pan. Place in the oven for 20 minutes to dry out and become slightly crisp. Set aside.

Soak the apricots in the brandy and ½ cup warm water for 20 minutes. Drain, reserving the soaking liquid, and set aside.

Use 1 tablespoon of the butter to grease a 4-quart slow cooker, greasing all the way up the sides of the insert. Place the bread cubes, apricots, and chocolate in the cooker and toss to combine.

In a medium bowl, whisk together the eggs, milk, cream, ½ cup of the sugar, the salt, and the apricot soaking liquid and stir until the sugar is almost dissolved. Pour the mixture over the ingredients in the cooker and push the bread cubes down into the liquid to completely cover them and even out the top. Generously dot the top with the remaining 2 tablespoons butter, then sprinkle with the remaining 1 teaspoon sugar, the cinnamon, and cacao nibs. Cook, covered, on the low setting for 3 to 4 hours. Turn off the heat and let the pudding rest while you prepare the Brandy Sauce. Spoon the pudding out onto individual plates, drizzle with the sauce, and serve.

Notes: If you're using the very dried-out apricots (usually those from California), you might need to soak them longer, until they're soft.

Cacao nibs are pieces of roasted shelled cacao beans. They're nice and crunchy, and have an intense chocolate flavor, but of course they aren't sweet at all. Scharffen Berger cacao nibs are available at some specialty food stores.

Makes about 1 cup

½ cup butter

1 cup sugar

½ cup brandy, or ¼ cup brandy
  plus ¼ cup water

¼ teaspoon ground cinnamon

⅛ teaspoon salt

1 large egg

2 tablespoons heavy cream

Brandy Sauce

In a 2-quart saucepan over medium heat, melt the butter. Add the sugar, brandy, cinnamon, and salt and whisk to combine. Cook at a simmer, whisking, until the sugar is dissolved and the mixture is light in color and foamy. Remove from the heat.

In a small bowl, beat the egg until frothy, then gradually whisk it into the mixture in the saucepan. Return the pan to medium heat and cook for about 2 minutes, stirring constantly, until thickened. Stir in the cream and remove from the heat. Keep at room temperature for up to 4 hours, until ready to use; or cover and refrigerate, then reheat in a microwave oven and stir in a few teaspoons of water to thin the sauce a bit.

SAKE PUNCH

Serves 8
4-quart slow cooker

1   tablespoon black tea leaves
2½ cups cheap sake
1   liter lychee juice (see Note)
2   teaspoons palm sugar or honey
1   lemon wedge
1   (1-inch) piece fresh ginger,
    peeled

The slow cooker is by far the most convenient way to serve hot drinks for a party: You simply put the ingredients in the cooker a couple of hours before the guests are due to arrive, turn the heat to high, and set out the mugs and a ladle for serving. The drink stays warm throughout the evening and you don't have to keep an eye on a pot on the stove (or replace Sternos under a chafing dish).

Put the tea leaves in a large tea ball and place it in a 4-quart slow cooker. Add all the remaining ingredients and cook, covered, on the high setting for 2 to 3 hours, or until the punch is bubbling around the edges. Ladle into small teacups, leaving the ginger and lemon behind, and serve straight from the slow cooker, set to warm. Remove the tea ball after 4 hours.

Note: Lychee juice can be found at many specialty or organic-food stores; the Ceres brand, sold in shelf-stable boxes, is widely available.

CARDAMOM-PEAR SPOON SWEET

Makes about 1½ cups
4-quart slow cooker

5   pears
    Juice of 1 lime
1   cup sugar
4   white or green cardamom pods
¼   teaspoon ground ginger
¼   teaspoon ground cinnamon
    Pinch of salt

I made this spoon sweet—like a compote—to accompany a hunk of good Manchego, a hard Spanish sheep's-milk cheese, but it would also pair well with other hard cheeses, like Idziabal, a smoky Spanish cow's-milk cheese, or, if you're lucky enough to find it, a true aged Asiago (vecchio) from the Trentino–Alto Adige in Italy. Or just spoon the pears onto toast and pretend it's jam.

Peel and core the pears, then cut them into ½-inch chunks. Put them in a 4-quart slow cooker and toss with the lime juice and sugar.

Using the side of a knife, crush the cardamom pods; discard the outer pods and crush the black seeds. Add the cardamom seeds, ginger, cinnamon, and salt to the cooker and toss to combine with the pears. Cook, covered, on the low setting for 8 to 10 hours (or on high for about 5 hours). Let cool to room temperature and serve, or store, tightly covered, in the refrigerator for up to 2 weeks.

ORANGE & PEACH MARMALADE

Makes about 2½ cups
4-quart slow cooker

3　navel oranges
1　lemon
1　peach
1　cup sugar
　　Pinch of salt

This is a fine simple refrigerator marmalade, excellent with hard cheeses as well as on sandwiches or toasted and buttered English muffins. It won't set into true jelly, though, unless you add a bit of fruit pectin (follow the directions on the package of pectin), but sometimes it will thicken substantially if you put lemon seeds in a small tea ball and add it to the cooker with the rest of the ingredients (discard the seeds after cooking).

Using the large holes of a box grater, coarsely grate the zest of the oranges (or remove the zest with a vegetable peeler and then cut it into julienne strips). Put the zest in a 4-quart slow cooker. Cut the white rind off the oranges and, slicing right next to the membrane separating each section and holding the oranges over the cooker insert to catch the juices, cut the sections out. Discard the membranes. Dice the oranges and very thinly slice the lemon and add them to the cooker.

Peel the peach by blanching it in boiling water for 3 minutes, then plunging it into ice water to loosen the skin. Remove the pit and dice the flesh. Add it to the slow cooker, along with the sugar, 1 cup water, and the salt, and stir to combine. Cook, covered, on the low setting for 6 to 8 hours, until the zest is soft and almost translucent and the liquid is thickened and bubbling; turn the cooker to high for the last 30 minutes of the cooking time. Transfer to clean jars and let cool to room temperature. The marmalade will keep, tightly covered in the refrigerator, for up to 2 weeks.

OLD-FASHIONED OATMEAL

Serves 4
4-quart slow cooker

2   cups steel-cut oats
    (not rolled oats)
½   teaspoon salt
2   tablespoons butter
4½ cups milk or water
    Fixings (see Note)

Put the ingredients in the slow cooker right before bed, and the oatmeal will be ready when you wake up six or eight hours later. It'll have a little crust around the edge of the cooker, but it sure beats stirring the stuff on the stovetop for 45 minutes first thing in the morning. Be sure you use old-fashioned steel-cut oats: Do not use rolled oats or anything that says "instant" on the package or you'll end up with mush.

Put the oats, salt, butter, and milk in a 4-quart slow cooker. If you're using raisins or other dried fruits, add them now (see Note). Cook, covered, on the low setting for 6 to 8 hours, until the oats are soft but still a bit chewy. Serve hot, with the fixings of your choice.

Note: Oatmeal is good served like grits, with a pat of butter and salt and pepper. Or pour some cold buttermilk, cream, or milk over it. Or stir in some raisins or dried cranberries or cherries when you put the oats in the slow cooker, then top the finished oatmeal with brown sugar and cinnamon and serve with milk.

OLD-FASHIONED APPLESAUCE

Makes 2½ to 3 pints
4-quart slow cooker

3   pounds red apples (7 or 8 medium apples)
¼   cup packed brown sugar
    Juice and grated zest of 1 lemon
2   sticks cinnamon, or 1 teaspoon good-quality ground cinnamon
¼   nutmeg, freshly grated
¼   teaspoon ground cloves (optional)

This classic applesauce is exceptionally easy to make using a slow cooker and a food mill. Applesauce made in a conventional pot on the stove must be stirred and watched carefully as it cooks to keep the apples from sticking to the pot and burning, but with a slow cooker you can simply load up the insert and walk away. A food mill is invaluable here as well: Not only does it eliminate the need to peel the apples, which is time-consuming and annoying, but cooking the apples with the peels on gives the applesauce a beautiful pink tint.

Any kind of red apple will work here, but I like a mixture of different varieties—tart and sweet, crisp eating apples and mealier baking apples—so that the finished texture is not as uniform as commercial applesauce and every bite is just slightly different.

Wash the apples and cut them into quarters; there's no need to peel them, but do cut out the cores if your food mill does not have a disk with very fine holes. Place the apples in a 4-quart slow cooker.

Combine all the remaining ingredients in a bowl with ½ cup water and stir to dissolve the brown sugar. Pour over the apples, stirring to coat them with the liquid. Cover the slow cooker and cook on the low setting for 4 hours, pushing the apples down into the liquid once or twice during the last hour of cooking.

Pass the apples through a stainless-steel food mill into a medium nonreactive bowl, using the disk with the finest holes, and discard the solids left in the food mill. Serve the applesauce warm, or let it cool to room temperature and chill, covered, in the refrigerator. It will keep in the refrigerator for about 1 week.

METRIC CONVERSION CHART

WEIGHT EQUIVALENTS

The metric weights given in this chart are not exact equivalents, but have been rounded up or down slightly to make measuring easier.

Avoirdupois	Metric
$\frac{1}{4}$ oz	7 g
$\frac{1}{2}$ oz	15 g
1 oz	30 g
2 oz	60 g
3 oz	90 g
4 oz	115 g
5 oz	150 g
6 oz	175 g
7 oz	200 g
8 oz ($\frac{1}{2}$ lb)	225 g
9 oz	250 g
10 oz	300 g
11 oz	325 g
12 oz	350 g
13 oz	375 g
14 oz	400 g
15 oz	425 g
16 oz (1 lb)	450 g
$1\frac{1}{2}$ lb	750 g
2 lb	900 g
$2\frac{1}{4}$ lb	1 kg
3 lb	1.4 kg
4 lb	1.8 kg

VOLUME EQUIVALENTS

These are not exact equivalents for American cups and spoons, but have been rounded up or down slightly to make measuring easier.

American	Metric	Imperial
$\frac{1}{4}$ t	1.2 ml	
$\frac{1}{2}$ t	2.5 ml	
1 t	5.0 ml	
$\frac{1}{2}$ T (1.5 t)	7.5 ml	
1 T (3 t)	15 ml	
$\frac{1}{4}$ cup (4 T)	60 ml	2 fl oz
$\frac{1}{3}$ cup (5 T)	75 ml	$2\frac{1}{2}$ fl oz
$\frac{1}{2}$ cup (8 T)	125 ml	4 fl oz
$\frac{2}{3}$ cup (10 T)	150 ml	5 fl oz
$\frac{3}{4}$ cup (12 T)	175 ml	6 fl oz
1 cup (16 T)	250 ml	8 fl oz
$1\frac{1}{4}$ cups	300 ml	10 fl oz ($\frac{1}{2}$ pt)
$1\frac{1}{2}$ cup	350 ml	12 fl oz
2 cups (1 pint)	500 ml	16 fl oz
$2\frac{1}{2}$ cups	625 ml	20 fl oz (1 pint)
1 quart	1 liter	32 fl oz

OVEN TEMPERATURE EQUIVALENTS

Oven Mark	F	C	Gas
Very cool	250–275	130–140	$\frac{1}{2}$ –1
Cool	300	150	2
Warm	325	170	3
Moderate	350	180	4
Moderately hot	375	190	5
	400	200	6
Hot	425	220	7
	450	230	8
Very hot	475	250	9

CREDITS & SOURCES

The following manufacturers and retailers generously provided equipment that was used in developing and testing the recipes contained in this book: All-Clad Metalcrafters; BonJour; Chicago Metallic Bakeware; Cuisinart; KitchenAid Home Appliances; Russell Hobbes; Waring Products, Inc.; and Williams-Sonoma.

ALL-CLAD METALCRAFTERS LLC
424 Morganza Road
Canonsburg, Pennsylvania 15317
Toll free: 1 (900) 255-2523
www.allclad.com
Known for their fine cookware, All-Clad makes a beautiful coffee urn for serving a crowd; their 7-quart, stainless-steel slow cooker can also be found at Williams-Sonoma stores and Williams-Sonoma.com.

BONJOUR, INC.
80 Berry Drive
Pacheco, California 94553
Toll free: 1 (800) 2-bonjour (226-6568)
www.bonjourproducts.com
BonJour features a complete line of kitchen tools and serving pieces.

CARRIBEAN ISLANDS GROCER
11624 Highway U.S.1
Sebastian, Florida 32958
Phone: (772) 589-9613
Fax: (772) 388-6568
www.caribbeanislandsgrocer.com
A global online grocery store specializing in traditional non-perishable Caribbean and West Indian specialty foods.

CHICAGO METALLIC, THE BAKEWARE COMPANY
120n Lakeview Parkway
Vernon Hills, Illinois 60061
www.bakingpans.com
The nonstick bakeware manufactured by Chicago Metallic makes for perfect baking and easy clean up.

CUISINART
Toll free: 1 (800) 726-0190
www.cuisinart.com
In addition to their famous food processors, look to Cuisinart for a full range of countertop appliances.

CULVER DUCK FARMS
P.O. Box 910
Middlebury, Indiana 46540
Toll free: 1 (800) 826-9225
www.culverduck.com
This family-owned company has raised quality ducklings for five
generations. Available at specialty food stores and for order online.

EL MERCADO GRANDE
Mesa, Arizona
Phone: (480) 862-2964
www.elmercadogrande.com
This online Latin superstore sells a wide variety of Central and
South American food products.

ETHNICGROCER.COM
695 Lunt Avenue
Elk Grove Village, Illinois 60007
Phone: (312) 373-1777
Fax: (312) 373-1777
www.ethnicgrocer.com
This online grocer sells food products from Asia, Southeast Asia, and
eastern and western Europe.

INDIAN FOODS COMPANY
8305 Franklin Avenue
Minneapolis, Minnesota 55426
Phone: (952) 593-3000
www.indianfoodsco.com
An online grocer with a complete pantry of Indian products.

KALUSTYAN'S
123 Lexington Avenue
New York, New York 10016
Toll free: 1 (800) 352-3451
www.kalustyans.com
Kalustyan's, the anchor of Manhattan's Little India neighborhood,
is one of my favorite stores in New York, and their website, though

the online prices are slightly higher, features an excellent selection of spices and specialty foods—look here for palm sugar, special honeys, masala spice mixes, Assam teas, and fancy juices and syrups. The spices are fresh and reasonably priced.

KITCHENAID
Countertop Appliance Information
P.O. Box 218
St. Joseph, Michigan 49085
Toll free: 1 (800) 541-6390
www.kitchenaid.com
KitchenAid manufactures a complete range of electric appliances both large and small.

MELISSA'S
World Variety Produce, Inc.
P.O. Box 21127
Los Angeles, California 90021
Toll free: 1 (800) 588-0151
www.melissas.com
The largest distributor of specialty produce in the United States, Melissa's is truly "one-stop shopping for the global marketplace."

NATIVE HARVEST
32033 East Round Lake Road
Ponsford, Minnesota 56575-3577
www.nativeharvest.com
Traditionally harvested wild rice, dried corn, and hominy as well as other natural food products.

NIMAN RANCH
1025 E. 12th St.
Oakland, California 94606
Phone: (866) 808-0340
www.nimanranch.com
Working with 300 independent family farmers, Niman Ranch sells organic beef, pork, and lamb at both specialty food stores and for order online.

PENZEYS SPICES
19300 West Janacek Court
Brookfield, Wisconsin 53008-0924
Toll-free: 1 (800) 741-7787
www.penzeys.com
This venerable mail-order spice purveyor's catalog is a cook's dream come true, and all of its products are available online.

RUSSELL HOBBS
Toll-free: 1 (888) HOBBS-20 (462-2720)
www.russell-hobbs.com
Russell Hobbs offers a slow cooker, immersion blenders, and other countertop appliances.

WARING PRODUCTS
314 Ella T. Grasso Avenue
Torrington, Connecticut 06790
Toll free: 1 (800) 4WARING (492-7464)
www.waringproducts.com
Specialists in blenders, the Waring line of countertop appliances includes juicers, drink mixers, coffeemakers, and an electric meat grinder.

WILLIAMS-SONOMA
3250 Van Ness Avenue
San Francisco, CA 94109
Toll-free: (877) 812-6235
www.williams-sonoma.com
There are more products available on the website of this fine-kitchen-wares retailer than the company features in its brick-and-mortar stores—look here for the very best slow cookers, food processors, blenders, other high-end appliances and kitchen utensils, and gourmet food products.

INDEX

Edited by Marisa Bulzone
Designed by Julie Hoffer
Graphic Production by Norman Watkins
Prop Stylist: Lynda White
Food Stylist: Michael Pederson

The text of this book was composed in Granjon and Myriad